CASE STUDIES IN
CULTURAL ANTHROPOLOGY

GENERAL EDITORS

George and Louise Spindler

STANFORD UNIVERSITY

THE OJIBWA OF BERENS RIVER,
MANITOBA
ETHNOGRAPHY INTO HISTORY

Frontispiece. Wooden bird figure and woman's decorated black velvet poncho, both formerly used in the Midewiwin ceremony, and collected by Hallowell for the Museum of the American Indian (Heye Foundation) in New York City. Most Midewiwin items that Hallowell collected from former practitioners were birch-bark scrolls and animal skin medicine bags; the poncho with its yarn, ribbons, and metal danglers, is entirely of traded materials.

THE OJIBWA OF BERENS RIVER, MANITOBA

ETHNOGRAPHY INTO HISTORY

A. IRVING HALLOWELL

edited
with Preface and Afterword
by
Jennifer S. H. Brown
University of Winnipeg

To Rayna Green – a very special colleague & friend – 15 Feb. 1992, Winnipeg – from Jennifer

Harcourt Brace Jovanovich College Publishers

FORT WORTH   NEW YORK   AUSTIN   PHILADELPHIA   SAN ANTONIO   SAN DIEGO
MONTREAL   TORONTO   LONDON   SYDNEY   TOKYO

Publisher	Ted Buchholz
Acquisitions Editor	Christopher P. Klein
Senior Project Editor	Charlie Dierker
Production Manager	Thomas Urquhart
Art & Design Supervisor	John Ritland

Library of Congress Cataloging-in-Publication Data

Hallowell, A. Irving (Alfred Irving) 1892–1974.
    The Ojibwa of Berens River, Manitoba : ethnography into history /
A. Irving Hallowell ; edited with preface and afterword by Jennifer
S. H. Brown.
      p.   cm. — (Case studies in cultural anthropology)
    Includes bibliographical references and index.
    ISBN 0-03-055122-6
    1. Ojibwa Indians—History. 2. Ojibwa Indians—Social life and
customs. 3. Ethnohistory—Manitoba—Berens River Valley. 4. Berens
River Valley (Man.)—History. 5. Berens River Valley (Man.)—Social
life and customs. I. Brown, Jennifer S. H., 1940– . II. Title.
III. Series.
E99.C6H26   1991
971.27'4—dc20   91-33538
                                               CIP

ISBN: 0-03-055122-6

Address for Editorial Correspondence
Harcourt Brace Jovanovich College Publishers, 301 Commerce Street, Suite 3700, Fort
Worth, TX 76102

Address for Orders
Harcourt Brace Jovanovich College Publishers, 6277 Sea Harbor Drive, Orlando, FL 32887
1-800-782-4479, or 1-800-433-0001 (in Florida)

Printed in the United States of America

2 3 4 5   016   9 8 7 6 5 4 3 2 1

Photo Credits

Cover photo, figures 1, 2, 3, 5, 6, 7, 8, 9, 10, 11, 13, 14, 15, 16, 17, 18, 19, 20, 22, 23—A.
I. Hallowell, courtesy of American Philosophical Society. Frontispiece courtesy of Museum
of the American Indian (Heye Foundation). Figure 4 courtesy of Stephen T. Boggs. Figure 12
courtesy of Cory Kilvert and Western Canada Pictorial Index, University of Winnipeg.
Figure 21 Western Canada Pictorial Index, University of Winnipeg.

Table of Contents

Foreword *George and Louise Spindler* vii
  About the Series vii
  About the Author vii
  About the Editor viii
  About this Case Study ix
Preface *Jennifer S. H. Brown*... xi
  Reviving a Case Study xi
  An Editor's Voice xii
  The Author's Life xiii
  Ethnography into History xiv
  Acknowledgments xvii
  List of Illustrations xix
  List of Maps xx

PART I   Historical Perspectives

Chapter 1   THE LIVING PAST IN THE CANADIAN WILDERNESS 3
  Voyage to Northern Manitoba 3
  Fieldwork with Chief William Berens 6
  History through the Berens Family 11

**Chapter 2   THE CANADIAN SHIELD, THE FUR TRADE, AND
            OJIBWA EXPANSION** 16
  Geography and Furs...16
  The Expansion of the Ojibwa 20
  Genealogical Evidence 22
  Trade Goods, Old and New...25

**Chapter 3   CHRISTIANIZATION, CONFEDERATION, AND
            TREATIES WITH THE INDIANS** 28
  The Missionaries...28
  Political Developments 30
  The Lake Winnipeg Treaty...32
  The New Order: Chiefs and Bands 35
  Subordination, Integration, and Continuity 37

PART II   Adaptation, Culture, and Religion

**Chapter 4   ECOLOGICAL ADAPTATION AND SOCIAL
            ORGANIZATION**..43
  Seasons and Subsistence 43
  Winter Hunting Groups 44
  Hunting Groups versus Hunting Territories..................................44

v

Summer Fishing Settlements 46
Kinship Patterns and Social Organization 50
Kinship Terms and Behavior 52
Avoidance, Joking, and Sweethearts 54
Marriage 56
Grandparents and "Our Grandfathers" 57

Chapter 5   WORLD VIEW AND BEHAVIORAL ENVIRONMENT 60
Animate and Inanimate 61
Other than Human Persons 63
Myth and Metamorphosis 65
The Shaking Tent 68
Causation and Cosmology 71
The Living and the Dead 74

Chapter 6   RELIGION, MORAL CONDUCT, AND PERSONALITY 80
A Culturally Constituted World 80
Seeking the Good Life 82
Dreams and Power 84
Dream Visitors and Fasting 87
Dream Experiences and Teachings 88
Dreaming and The Moral Order 91
Blessings, Illness, and Confession 92
Self-Reliance and Moral Responsibility 96
Personality in Culture 97

Appendix   DWELLINGS AND HOUSEHOLDS ALONG THE
BERENS RIVER [1935–36] 100
Housing: Adopted Forms 100
Aboriginal Dwellings 102
Household Composition 107

Afterword   *Jennifer S. H. Brown* 111
An Ethnography of Experience 111
Hallowell and the Living Past 112
Situating the Berens Family 112
"Tackling the Women" 113
Ethnography as History 115

References 116

Index 122

Foreword

ABOUT THE SERIES

These Case Studies in Cultural Anthropology (CSCA) are designed for students in beginning and intermediate courses in the social sciences, to bring them insights into the richness and complexity of human life as it is lived in different ways, in different places. The authors are men and women who have lived in the societies they write about and who are professionally trained as observers and interpreters of human behavior. Also, the authors are teachers; in their writing, the needs of the student reader remain foremost. It is our belief that when students gain an understanding of ways of life very different from their own, abstractions and generalizations about the human condition become meaningful.

The scope and character of the series has changed continually since we published the first case studies in 1960. We are concerned with ways in which human groups and communities are coping with the massive changes wrought in their physical and social environments in recent decades. We are also concerned with the ways in which established cultures have met life's problems. We also want to include representation of the various modes of communication and emphasis that are being formed and reformed as anthropology itself changes.

We think of the CSCA as an instructional series, intended for use in the classroom. We have always used case studies in our teaching, whether for neophytes or advanced graduate students. We start with case studies, whether from our own series or from elsewhere, and weave our way into theory, and then turn again to cases. For us, they are the grounding of our discipline.

ABOUT THE AUTHOR
A. IRVING HALLOWELL (1892–1974)

The editor of this case study, Jennifer S. H. Brown of the University of Winnipeg, introduces both the author, A. I. Hallowell, and the unusual circumstances surrounding the publication of this volume, in her Preface. We can add a few comments reflecting our own relationship to Hallowell and his work, for our relationship was like that of many others.

"Pete" Hallowell, as he was known to his many colleagues and students, was, and still is, one of the most influential figures in American anthropology. His interests and publications range with impressive breadth through the history of anthropology; Indian–white relations; the impact of the fur trade on northern peoples; the distribution of cultural complexes, such as bear ceremonialism in the circumpolar regions; the ethnography of the Cree and Ojibwa; adaptations to the changing circumstances of life in these societies; the culturally constituted aspects of personality, self, and person; and the use of projective techniques in the cross-cultural study of psychological adaptation and adjustment. It is these last two categories that provided our most important links with him, both as aspiring graduate students and as mature professionals.

Like so many others, we were profoundly influenced by Hallowell before we knew him personally. When we were in graduate school at the University of Wisconsin at Madison (1945–1948), his studies of the acculturation of the Ojibwa quickly became models for us. His analysis of the psychological adaptations of the Ojibwa at three different levels of sociocultural change were the point of departure for our study of the Menominee, also Algonquians, that has been a major pre-occupation in our professional lives.

The first time we met him was at the American Anthropological Association meetings in Philadelphia in 1952, where we presented some preliminary findings of our Menominee research on psychological adaptation and culture change. Pete, who was there as discussant of that section of the program, praised our work, humbly declared it to be more precise and more carefully designed than his (on similar relationships among the Ojibwa), and pointed out some subtle phenomena that we had only partially anticipated. From that time on, Pete was a major influence on our lives and emerging professionalism. We saw him infrequently but exchanged papers and correspondence, and we read avidly everything he published.

As Jennifer Brown describes in her Preface, in 1962 we invited Hallowell to write a case study on the Ojibwa for our then emerging series, Case Studies in Cultural Anthropology. Actually he was one of the first colleagues we contacted when we began to think about the series in the late 1950s, but his contract with Holt, Rinehart and Winston was not finalized until 1962. The manuscript was slow in coming. Pete had a lot of irons in the fire and he was not as young at 72 years of age as we thought he was (he seemed ageless to us). The loss of the finished manuscript by Railway Express en route from Pennsylvania to California was unbearable, and Pete, disheartened by the loss, did not return to it again.

We did not know of the existence of an earlier draft of the case study until Jennifer Brown contacted us at the American Anthropological Association meetings in Washington, D. C. in November 1989. She had found the draft in Hallowell's papers in the archives of the American Philosophical Society in Philadelphia. We are particularly grateful to her for her discovery of the manuscript and her diligent and knowledgeable editing of it.

ABOUT THE EDITOR

Jennifer S. H. Brown is a professor of history at the University of Winnipeg in Winnipeg, Canada. Born in Providence, Rhode Island, of Canadian parents, she earned her B.A. from Brown University, a master's degree from Harvard, and her Ph.D. in anthropology from the University of Chicago. She first developed an interest in ethnohistory while studying colonial Spanish documents in Peru. From the 1970s onward, her studies have focused on Northern Algonquian peoples and their relations with fur traders, missionaries, and (through the research for this book) anthropologists.

Her publications include *Strangers in Blood: Fur Trade Company Families in Indian Country* (1980); *The New Peoples: Being and Becoming Métis in North America* (1985), coedited with Jacqueline Peterson; *The Orders of the Dreamed: George Nelson on Cree and Northern Ojibwa Religion and Myth, 1823* (1988), with Robert Brightman; and over 60 articles and reviews. She is a past president of the American Society for Ethnohistory, and recently was awarded a five-year Social Sciences and Humanities Research Council of Canada research grant to study subarctic native historical perspectives on the fur trade, 1750–1950. She and her husband, Wilson B. Brown, an economist at the University of Winnipeg, have resided in Winnipeg since 1983. They and their son, Matthew, have long enjoyed northern summers on an island near Parry Sound, Ontario.

ABOUT THIS CASE STUDY

This case study of the Ojibwa of Berens River, Manitoba is an excellent example of Pete Hallowell's intellectual breadth. Part I combines ethnohistorical, ecological, ethnographic, and sociopolitical analyses into a comprehensive treatment of the situation of the Berens River Ojibwa over time. Part II continues with an ecological orientation in Chapter 4, "Ecological Adaptation and Social Organization," and moves directly into residential groups, kinship, and marriage. The treatment of kinship is especially gratifying. Kin terminology and behavior are effectively joined so that the use of kin terms becomes a social process and not an abstraction.

Chapters 5 and 6 are, to us, "pure Hallowell." Chapter 5, "World View and Behavioral Environment," presents the essentials of how the Ojibwa conceive of the place of humans in their universe, and particularly how humans and "other than humans" constitute concepts of "person" and self that are radically different from Western concepts of such. The boundaries between animal and human are not sharply drawn in Ojibwa culture, so the concept of person is more inclusive and more fluid than in Western culture. Hallowell makes the point, in this context and elsewhere, that any attempt to use such Western categories as "animal," "human," "supernatural," or even "religion" inevitably distorts the Ojibwa world view, although he uses the term *religion* in the title of Chapter 6 to communicate what the chapter is about from a Western point of view. Hallowell struggled with the problems of cultural translation that dog all scholars trying to communicate the nature of one culture to readers from another.

Chapter 6, "Religion, Moral Conduct, and Personality," carries the arguments begun in Chapter 5 to their conclusion in a "culturally constituted world" in which dreams as sources of power, of teaching, and of moral order are central processes. Again, fundamental differences from a Western culturally constituted world become apparent. The boundary between "dream" and "reality" that is basic to Western thinking, especially psychiatric and psychoanalytic thinking, is a highly permeable one in the Ojibwa world view.

Hallowell scarcely mentions, in this case study, his extensive and pioneering use of the Rorschach inkblot projective technique to explore the perceptual and personality differences between Ojibwa populations that are characterized by different degrees of adaptation to the impact of Western culture. This research was a major source of inspiration to us and we have recently reviewed and reevaluated our Menominee researches using this technique in the light of Hallowell's findings. "Rorschaching in North America in the Shadow of Hallowell" is published in a special issue of the journal *The Psychoanalytic Study of Society* (1991) dedicated to Hallowell. This journal is edited by Bryce Boyer, who along with his wife, Ruth Boyer, has long been a devotee of projective techniques in cross-cultural research.

This aspect of Hallowell's work is least understood or appreciated among anthropologists, many of whom are "psychophobic." Although psychological anthropology is a respectable subdivision of sociocultural anthropology, at least in some quarters, any "reduction" to psychological processes and any use of psychological techniques such as the Rorschach test are regarded with a certain antipathy. Hallowell was interested, as we are, in processes of psychological adaptation and adjustment cross culturally. His use of the Rorschach test is just one more indication of his driving intellectual curiosity. He was indeed a man for all seasons.

Hallowell anticipated, as Jennifer Brown points out in her Afterword, certain current trends in interpretive anthropology, particularly those centering on concepts of personhood, ideas about the cultural construction of the self, and the expression of emotions. His Chapter 6 in this study, first published as an article in 1960, is clear evidence of the degree to which these concerns had become important to him some years before they were enunciated by the "postmodernists." And yet, he is nowhere cited by these writers. Rather, they credit Clifford Geertz with initiating the interest in the 1970s in the cultural definition of the person as a focus of ethnography. Other evidence of the pioneering quality of Hallowell's thinking is discussed in Jennifer Brown's Afterword, which, for some readers, might well be read first, rather than last.

Lastly, we are fortunate to have, as an appendix to this case study, "Dwellings and Households along the Berens River." Hallowell drafted this section for an unfinished manuscript, *Pigeon River People,* written in 1935–1936. Its text and photos give us a realistic view of the environment and habitations of the Ojibwa in the 1930s and some sense of the changes that were taking place during the period immediately before Hallowell started his fieldwork. Hallowell's interest in these dwellings and the rich ethnohistorical detail he provides about them are also evidence of his broad-ranging concern to record and understand all aspects of Berens River life and culture to the best of his ability.

GEORGE AND LOUISE SPINDLER
Ethnographics, Calistoga, California

Preface

REVIVING A CASE STUDY

This book has several layers in its different parts and in its origins. In the decade from 1930 to 1940, A. Irving "Pete" Hallowell made a series of seven summer fieldwork visits to Berens River Ojibwa communities in Manitoba and northwestern Ontario. In about 1935–1936, he drafted parts of a monograph, *Pigeon River People,* which he evidently intended as a comprehensive ethnography of Berens River. The Appendix in this volume, on dwellings and households, is adapted from a section of that draft, which he set aside as he pursued new lines of psychological analysis in the late 1930s and 1940s. Parts I and II (Chapters 1–6) are the edited draft chapters of Hallowell's original Case Studies in Cultural Anthropology text, written in the mid-1960s, which survived the loss of the completed manuscript en route to Holt, Rinehart and Winston in 1967.

Hallowell had begun to think about the Case Studies project in September of 1962, upon being invited by George and Louise Spindler to undertake the preparation of a volume on the Ojibwa for that series — new at the time. They proposed a book that would convey "the essential qualities and patterns of Ojibwa culture as you have so admirably described them," and added, "As we have thought about the Ojibwa, as you have acquainted us with them, we could think of no case study we would rather have." Pete Hallowell's favorable response led to a contract being issued that November.

Editors often endure missed deadlines, and Hallowell's correspondence files contain several queries from George Spindler on the progress of the book over the next five years. Finally in November 1967, a letter from Spindler recorded the fate of the finished text: "We are devastated to learn of the loss, temporary we hope, of the carton by Railway Express containing . . . the corrected manuscript of the Ojibwa book."[1] The shipment was never found, and the Spindlers' subsequent encouragements to Hallowell to reconstruct the lost text asked more than his declining health allowed. He died on October 10, 1974, without returning to the project. Losing a manuscript in such a way was perhaps more likely in 1967 than now, with all our photocopiers and computer disks. But it usefully warns us all to keep copies in some form of any text that we value.

The draft chapters, which were already well organized and well written, have been lightly edited for style and clarity. Some details of Canadian history have been silently corrected, and some further examples and quotations have been added from Hallowell's research notes and unpublished writings to make the presentation more concrete and accessible. The Preface and Afterword, citations of sources in the text,

---

[1] The story of Hallowell's work on the case study and of its loss emerges from partially preserved correspondence between Hallowell and the Spindlers, and Hallowell and Holt, Rinehart and Winston, in the Hallowell papers in the American Philosophical Society in Philadelphia.

chapter endnotes, References, and most subheads are my editorial additions. Hallowell typically documented his finished works with ample references and footnotes, and my emendations are meant to respect what he would have wished to cite if he were finishing the job. Because the in-text references represent my additions, the customary parentheses surrounding them have been replaced by square brackets [thus], in accord with documentary publishing conventions for marking added material, except in the rare instances where Hallowell had included citations. The photographs in this book, unless otherwise credited, are Hallowell's own, taken in the 1930s and previously unpublished.

AN EDITOR'S VOICE

Any author's text, if looked at with care, reveals layers of memory, growth, recasting of presentation, and mediation by others. The checkered history of this book, unique in the Case Studies series, simply represents in exaggerated form what every book (and author) goes through as a text is revised, criticized by editors and specialist readers, and then reedited by the author and by professionals working for the publisher. What is unusual about this volume is that its gestation was more elephantine and the phases of its development more visible in the final product. It evolved over five decades, from Hallowell's initial tinkerings with *Pigeon River People* to the present book, which greets the world almost two decades after the author's death.

Readers of any book, and of a posthumous book in particular, are entitled to know something of the midwifery process that brings it forth, as well as of its parentage and lineage. Since the subjective experience and personal research interests of two parties, the author and the editor, have converged in this enterprise, a retrospective look at how they came together (although we never met) seems in order. After all, every book is at least to some degree autobiographical, whether on an implicit or explicit level.

I first encountered Hallowell's work sometime in the late 1960s, not long before I acquired the paperback edition (1967) of his collected essays, *Culture and Experience* (1955). I recall reading passages from that book to students at Colby College, and then at Northern Illinois University, to make points about cultural constructions of reality and about perception. But my interest in Berens River had family roots too. My father's maternal grandfather was Egerton R. Young, the first missionary at Berens River in 1873–1876. Young knew Jacob Berens, and he and his wife witnessed the signing of Treaty 5 (1875) by Berens and others. As a boy, William Berens (Hallowell's principal informant and collaborator) would have played with Young's eldest son, Eddie (later the Rev. E. Ryerson Young), at Berens River, and contributed to Eddie's brief assimilation into the Indian community—rich in implications and vividly recollected in a memoir that Eddie wrote as an old man in the 1950s (Brown 1987b).

Nineteenth-century missionaries, whether ancestral or not, often seem as complex and inaccessible to later scholarly understanding as the native "others" in which anthropologists have specialized. The Ojibwa–Methodist meeting at Berens

River, resonating through my father's memories of his grandfather and through Hallowell's absorption with Berens family history, afforded one of my personal initiations into the field of ethnohistory, with its focused attention on rereadings of documents, mediation processes in texts and memories, and the complex cultural constructions that natives and newcomers in centuries of encounters have elaborated around each other and themselves.

When I undertook doctoral studies at the University of Chicago in 1970, Hallowell became a kind of intellectual grandfather to me. Two of my professors, Raymond Fogelson and George W. Stocking, Jr., had studied with Hallowell at the University of Pennsylvania, and his influence on them was unmistakable. Hallowell's writings on the history of anthropology (see Chapters 2–4 in Hallowell 1976) find more than echoes in Stocking's work. And Fogelson passes on to his students a strong Hallowellian interest in the fine-tuned analysis of cultural categories, world view, and concepts of the person and the self—all contextualized and enriched through field, archival, and documentary research. In the early 1970s, Fogelson urged me to find a way to meet Hallowell, the mentor he sometimes addressed as "Uncle Pete." But younger people often assume their elders will be there almost any time, and wait too long. Hallowell died at the age of 81 before I could follow Fogelson's advice.

THE AUTHOR'S LIFE

Some scholars are fortunate in the early advantages they receive from parents and grandparents, familial and intellectual; others find paths towards achievement later and more on their own. Hallowell was of the latter category. He was born on December 28, 1892 in Philadelphia, the only child of parents who were also natives of that city.[2] His father, who had no postsecondary education, worked for Philadelphia shipbuilding companies; his mother graduated from the local "normal school" for girls, and taught school until she married. She had social and educational aspirations for her son. As Hallowell later recalled, "I realize now I was looked after too much, not only because I was an only child but mother had her own ideas and she was anxious to bring me up in the right way." The family lived with Hallowell's father's parents, and later with his widowed grandmother who was seemingly closer to her grandson than to her daughter-in-law, to whom she left most household duties. Possibly these familial dynamics later helped draw Hallowell to anthropology and psychology as fields that contributed towards understanding such relationships.

A childhood turning point was Hallowell's rebellion against entering Philadelphia Central High School, which required Latin and other difficult subjects, and his move, supported by his mechanically inclined father, to attend a manual training

[2] Published biographical information on Hallowell is available in the Introduction and Chapter 1 of Hallowell 1976, in Melford Spiro's obituary (1976), and in A.F.C. Wallace's biography (1980). I have added here some further personal data from the 1951 interview material assembled by Ann Roe when she selected Hallowell as one of the subjects for her book, *The Making of a Scientist;* the transcript had been sealed until my 1990 visit to the American Philosophical Society, which holds her papers.

school instead. As he told biographer Ann Roe in 1951, "it was a new building and they had a swell mandolin club." He enjoyed the school but found that neither his interests nor his skills lay in drafting, woodworking, and the like. Unprepared for a regular university program, he followed his mother's advice to go to the Wharton School for a degree in business, and there found himself most interested not in business, but in economics and sociology, reform and pacifism. Upon graduating in 1914, Hallowell became a social worker for eight years while taking graduate courses in sociology.

Anthropology first drew Hallowell's attention through his friendship with Frank Speck, a fellow member of his college fraternity, who specialized in northeastern Algonquian peoples and was trying to build up the anthropology program at the University of Pennsylvania. Speck, as Hallowell remembered him, "was the kind of fellow that loved to have people hanging around and talking to him," and as a result, "a lot of stuff rubbed off outside of the regular classwork." Hallowell took a master's degree in anthropology in 1920 and received his doctorate in 1924, working with Speck and also having studied more briefly with Alexander Goldenweiser and with Franz Boas at Columbia University. His dissertation, far-reaching both historically and comparatively, was a study of bear ceremonialism in the Northern Hemisphere (Hallowell 1926).

From the early 1920s until his retirement in 1962, three years excepted, Hallowell taught anthropology at the University of Pennsylvania. During the 1920s, he had some limited field experience under Speck's guidance and ranged widely across his chosen discipline in his teaching and research. His 1930 field trip to study the Swampy Cree of northern Manitoba, Canada was, however, his first venture beyond the range of Speck's northeastern studies. Chapter 1 of the present book recounts how Hallowell came to Manitoba with Cree studies in mind and then through the agency of William Berens was drawn to spend the next and most formative decade of his professional career on Ojibwa ethnography. It was in doing that work that he found his niche, applying his wide-ranging knowledge and his analytical skills to the study of a broad spectrum of topics growing out of the data that he and Berens gathered.

Perhaps his most pioneering and experimental research was the application of the Rorschach inkblot test to the analysis of Ojibwa personality structure, an exploration that led also, in the 1940s and early 1950s, to the gathering of comparative test data from the Lac du Flambeau Ojibwa (Chippewa) of Wisconsin. Readers of this book may notice that in it Hallowell refers only once to the Rorschach test. Although the results of its use were suggestive, his analyses of Ojibwa people and their lives found their best expression in the textured prose of his articles, numbers of which have become classics in cultural anthropology.

ETHNOGRAPHY INTO HISTORY

The subtitle of this book (which is an editorial addition) draws attention to several points. First, it alludes to the dynamics of Hallowell's intellectual development and shifting perspectives as his Berens River experience became a part of his personal past. For anthropologists, or travelers generally, the immediacy of fieldwork (or of any sojourn abroad) is layered over by time, distance, reflection, and selective memory. The quality of the experience is changed. Returning to his subculture of anthropology and university teaching in Philadelphia, Hallowell brought the Berens River Ojibwa into his own culturally constituted world (to borrow his phraseology) and increasingly placed them in a broad analytical and comparative perspective. The scope of his interests in such areas as culture and personality and human behavioral evolution may in fact have made it more difficult for him, in his later years, to concentrate on completing a focused ethnographic study of the Berens River Ojibwa, whether in the form of *Pigeon River People* or in the Case Studies format.

His interests were changing in another direction, too, from the mid-1950s onward. It was in the last 15 years of his publishing career (1957–1972) that he produced several important essays with a conspicuously historical slant, on the history of American anthropology and on Indian–white relations (see the papers reprinted in Hallowell 1976: Chapters 1–4 and 12–13). His data collecting in the 1930s and some of his earlier writings, notably "Some Psychological Characteristics of the Northeastern Indians" (in Hallowell 1955, first published in 1946), had already demonstrated a strong interest in history, which found expression, as well, in his work on acculturation as historical process. But this interest became more explicit near the end of his career.

As applied to the Ojibwa, his shift towards history appears most marked in the book published here, and in fact it generates a certain structural problem for the text viewed as a whole. The first three chapters are entirely historical and have, at points, a certain romantic quality as exploration narrative, as Hallowell describes his voyage into "the living past in the Canadian wilderness" and his growing friendship with Chief Berens, under whose influence "I became historically oriented as a matter of course" (Chapter 1). Hallowell's correspondence with Holt, Rinehart and Winston shows that he wrote Chapters 1–3 within a year of signing the contract for the book. These chapters were a new, fresh synthesis emphasizing historical processes and events, and they also gave him the chance to bring forth data on the history of William Berens' family which he had not previously organized to any great extent.

It was Chapters 4–6, then, that progressed slowly over the next four years. There were practical reasons for delay; as he wrote to the publisher in an undated letter (November 1963?) requesting a deadline extension, his retirement had left him with less income than expected and hence with a need to take on added teaching and consulting. But it may also have become difficult for him to focus creatively on those chapters' materials, which he had already worked up at length in prior publications, and which did not afford the historical dimensions that attracted him in the 1960s. The result is some disjuncture between Chapters 1–3 and 4–6 in both subject and approach. Another consequence is a problem with verb tense. In the first chapters, the past tense is almost universal, and appropriate. In Chapters 4–6, the venerable anthropological convention of writing in the ahistorical ethnographic present vies with the presenting of data recorded in and often specific to the 1930s. Hallowell's drafts themselves reveal his revisings of tense at various points.

To resolve this editorial question, consistency has been sought within paragraphs, and the past tense is maintained where the text clearly pertains to people and experiences of the 1930s. But the issue is, of course, more than editorial. It raises basic questions about the presentation of ethnographic data, particularly data that have become "historicized" by the passage of several decades. What aspects of Berens River Ojibwa world view, values, and experience recorded in the 1930s are valid in the 1990s such that they may still be expressed in the present tense? People change, find new values, blend the old and the new, or return with vigor to (re)constructing the old. Ojibwa individuals and communities are pursuing all these options at present in both Canada and the United States.

Nor can we arbitrarily cast Hallowell's generalizations into a past tense that reinforces older writers' myth of the Disappearing Indian. In sum, the tense problem in anthropological writings, particularly as they age, cries out for attention, and symbolizes, too, how little we really know or can assume. To suppress it editorially in this book would be to suppress larger issues that demand the continuing awareness of both students and scholars.

Another question that anthropologists must deal with in a thoughtful, sensitive way is the matter of identifying the communities and people who provided their data. Issues and perspectives change as ethnographies pass into history and as anthropology itself evolves. Hallowell never disguised the locale of his work, although he was often circumspect about referring to individuals. William Berens was sometimes thinly disguised as, for example, "W. B." or "my informant." But Hallowell dedicated his important monograph on Saulteaux (Ojibwa) conjuring (1942) to Berens "whose genial companionship in camp and canoe, in fair weather and foul, never failed to enliven my task"; and Berens appears front and center in Chapter 1 of this book, as a historical figure in his own right. And he not only gave permission as chief for Hallowell to work among his people; he invited him to come. Much of the time, he showed considerable sympathy and understanding for what the anthropologist was trying to do (but see Brown 1989:220–222 for some difficult moments).

Historians and archivists handling recent data and documents often apply a 25- or 30-year rule to the release of personal names and information. The transcript of each biographical interview that Ann Roe recorded with her scientist subjects, including Hallowell, was sealed until 10 years after the subject's death. There is a scholarly convention, then, that personal data should be privileged for some period, variously defined, and may then be made accessible—although clearly some materials remain highly sensitive longer than others. Cases vary, and each requires discretion and caution.

One argument in favor of historicizing ethnographic data after due passage of time is to allow these materials to contribute to their subjects' own histories and heritage and to bring about an honest return to communities of information and interpretations carried away by former visitors. Historically specific materials thereby become usable by the people from whom they came, who may then also evaluate and criticize them and the resulting analyses. In the 1960s, the chances of Berens River people reading this book would have been low, no matter what its historical usefulness or interest; William Berens had died in 1947, and Hallowell had lost touch with his other acquaintances in the area. In the 1990s, some readers will be from the communities that Hallowell visited, and they will have their own range of views about the quality and uses of his work as both anthropology and history. Some may travel to Philadelphia to consult his field notes and other manuscripts (open to any serious researcher) in the American Philosophical Society library in that city, or they may examine (in the Museum of the American Indian in New York, soon to be moved to Washington, D. C.) the numerous artifacts and ceremonial items that Hallowell obtained from descendants of Berens River Midewiwin (Grand Medicine Society) practitioners because the ceremony was no longer being carried on in the area. They may place Hallowell's materials in new historical contexts for their own purposes.

Some Berens River people, in any case, have already historicized Hallowell in their traditions. Some descendants of Chief Berens remember him showing those funny pictures (the Rorschach test) and his efforts (sometimes strained, as he knew) to elicit responses. A recent resident among the upriver people, Gary Butikofer, found that they remembered him by the name, *Atisokewinini,* or "myth man," because he was always asking for stories, and out-of-season in some instances too, since traditionally the *atisokanak,* or myths about other than human beings, were not to be told in summer. The name probably has a double meaning. Hallowell was also a teller of stories, trying to explain his activities and the curious world that he came from. The anthropologist himself became, reciprocally, a subject of study and speculation by his subjects, an event in their history.

ACKNOWLEDGMENTS

In November of 1989, a brief talk with George and Louise Spindler at the American Anthropological Association meetings in Washington, D. C., led me to propose to them the revival of a case study that had seemed a lost cause since 1967. Their encouragement was a source of great help, and their enthusiasm seemed contagious as Holt, Rinehart and Winston quickly lent support to the project. The American Philosophical Society, holder of Hallowell's papers, kindly gave permission for publication of the surviving manuscript drafts and of the Hallowell photographs that accompany this text, and I am grateful to Dr. Edward C. Carter II, the society's secretary, for that permission.

Other parties played considerable roles in making possible the background research that prepared me to respond to the Spindlers' encouragement. In 1986 and again in 1990, I received small research grants from the University of Winnipeg, funded by the Social Sciences and Humanities Research Council of Canada, to do research in Hallowell's papers. I owe special thanks to the manuscripts librarians at the American Philosophical Society, Beth Carroll-Horrocks and Martin Levitt, for their knowledgeable and patient assistance during my visits. At the Museum of the American Indian (Heye Foundation) in New York, James G. E. Smith and his staff facilitated my searches for Hallowell's Cree and Ojibwa materials. The Museum kindly arranged to photograph some items for study and for use in this book. The Hudson's Bay Company Archives, Provincial Archives of Manitoba, was, as always, an unparalleled resource on the fur trade and Berens River history; Hallowell would envy the ease of access that its current research visitors now enjoy.

Raymond D. Fogelson of the University of Chicago has taken a continuing interest in my work on Hallowell, and I have greatly appreciated his suggestions and ideas. When I discovered that a slightly edited version of Chapter 4 had already appeared (as Chapter 8 in Hallowell 1976), he and the University of Chicago Press were quick to arrange permission for the reprinting of the text. The staff of the Hudson's Bay Company Archives, Provincial Archives of Manitoba, were most helpful in pursuing sometimes obscure Berens River materials, as was my diligent research assistant, Erica Smith. Thora Cooke, senior researcher at the Western Canada Pictorial Index at the University of Winnipeg, made her knowledge and Index resources fully available to me in the search for pictorial data on Berens River. Linda Gladstone, secretary of the department of history at the university, patiently did the word processing of the Hallowell chapters from hand-written manuscript to final text.

Beginning some years ago, various individuals have contributed importantly to my still partial knowledge and understanding of the people and history of Berens River. My father, Harcourt Brown, and his cousin, the Reverend H. Egerton Young, through their family memories and papers, made Berens River and the Reverend E. R. Young into far more than names. Maurice Berens, grandson of Chief Berens and honours history graduate of the University of Winnipeg, combined course research and family history to bring to both him and me a better understanding of his grandfather and his community; I am grateful to him and to other family members he consulted for the knowledge they have shared.

Mary Black-Rogers freely shared her vast knowledge of the Ojibwa of northwestern Ontario, even if I sometimes failed to answer her questions or follow all the lines of inquiry she suggested. Gary Butikofer, who has resided for almost two decades at Poplar Hill and Red Lake, Ontario and has worked to identify Hallowell's photographs and to record the local and family history of the region, has been of immense help in documenting a number of the illustrations in this book. On the lower reaches of Berens River, Ken Vipond and Raymond Beaumont have contributed their considerable first-hand knowledge and contacts to the answering of queries and clarifying of details. In 1990, I was gratified by the willingness of Stephen Boggs, professor emeritus at the University of Hawaii, to share his experiences and photographs dating from the summer of 1952, which he spent at Berens River doing graduate research. In turn, his acquaintance that summer with Cory Kilvert, a professional photographer, led me (with Thora Cooke's help) to meet Kilvert, who has freely shared with us his images of Berens River and other northern communities from the 1940s and 1950s.

Finally, family members and particular friends have lent me their usual support, helpful commentaries, and intellectual stimulation, even if in some instances we do not meet often enough. And although I cannot claim to know whom Hallowell would have acknowledged for his part, two persons would surely stand out in his mind. First, William Berens, who in fundamental ways made this book possible. Second, Maude Frame Hallowell, a scholar in her own right, who also gave great personal and professional support to her husband over more than three decades of his life and who preserved and organized his papers with future researchers in mind.

Jennifer S. H. Brown

List of Illustrations

Frontispiece. Wooden bird figure and woman's black velvet Midewiwin poncho

Figure   1. The S. S. Keenora *and the* Wolverine *docked at Berens River.* 7

Figure   2. Chief William Berens and his family. 7

Figure   3. Traveling on the Berens River. 9

Figure   4. John Keeper, William Berens, A. I. Hallowell, and Antoine Bittern. ... 10

Figure   5. Making a rabbit-skin blanket. 19

Figure   6. Stretching a hide. 19

Figure   7. Summer fishing settlement in the Little Grand Rapids area. 48

Figure   8. Chief William Berens and "our grandfather's rock." 58

Figure   9. Constructing a shaking tent. 69

Figure 10. The shaking tent upon completion. 69

Figure 11. Wabano pavilion. 75

Figure 12. Graves at Little Grand Rapids. 76

Figure 13. Drummers and drum for Nämawin's drum dance. 77

Figure 14. Pavilion used in Nämawin's drum dance. 78

Figure 15. Nämawin (Fair Wind). 83

Figure 16. John Duck and his Wabano pavilion. 84

Figure 17. Dream chart. 86

Figure 18. Tent and log house at Little Grand Rapids. 101

Figure 19. Pí'kogan at Little Grand Rapids. 103

Figure 20. Wáginogan framework. 104

Figure 21. Cäbandawan on the lower Red River, 1858. 106

Figure 22. The Keeper family dwelling, Little Grand Rapids. 107

Figure 23. House of Chief William Berens and his family. 109

List of Maps

Map 1. The Cree-Ojibwa country of northwestern Ontario and Manitoba. 2
Map 2. Locations and movements of the major Berens River patrilineages. 23
Map 3. The Berens River Indian Reserve at the mouth of the river. 34
Map 4. Lake Pikangikum summer settlement, 1932. 47

PART ONE

HISTORICAL PERSPECTIVES

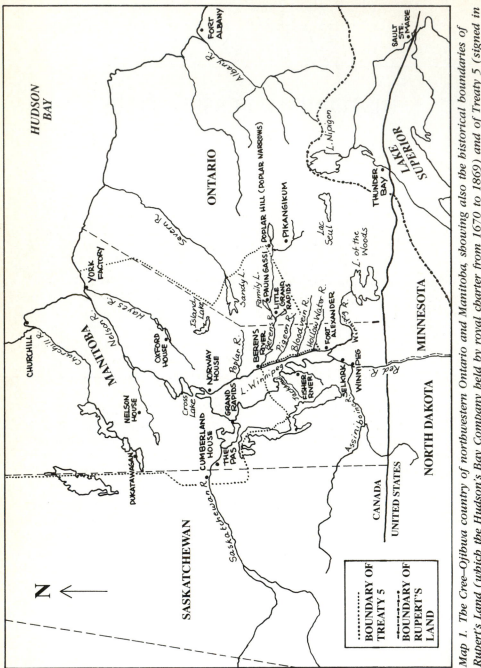

Map 1. The Cree–Ojibwa country of northwestern Ontario and Manitoba, showing also the historical boundaries of Rupert's Land (which the Hudson's Bay Company held by royal charter from 1670 to 1869) and of Treaty 5 (signed in 1875). (Map drawn by Erica Smith)

1 / The Living Past in the Canadian Wilderness

As more and more radical political, economic, social, and cultural changes sweep the world, a historical framework for ethnographic description and analysis is more than ever necessary. This is particularly the case when dealing with the Indians of the northern coniferous forest region of Canada, whose destiny has involved them so inextricably with the fur trade and the history of the Dominion itself. As Edward S. Rogers has pointed out, "they cannot be analysed, examined, or described as have been many, if not most, non-literate peoples. A different frame of reference must be adopted, taking into consideration this interdependence with Canadian society. At almost every point, understanding of their way of life is only possible when it is viewed against a backdrop of Euro-Canadian contact. . . . It is foolhardy to attempt to study these people as though they lived in a vacuum" [Rogers 1962:6]. This is doubly desirable in the present case, for many changes have taken place since the fieldwork on which this monograph is based was initiated.

It is likewise historically relevant for the reader to have some knowledge of the personal sources from which the observer derived his information. I have given considerable prominence here to one of my chief informants, William Berens, and his family, because in his direct ancestry there were persons who exemplified in microcosm the kinds of changes that were occurring among the Indians over a wide area, simultaneously with a tendency towards conserving the native culture of the past. The life histories of William Berens' forebears, as well as that of Berens himself, exhibit the historical process in concrete and personal form. This is a page often left blank because the Indians themselves left no records which can be correlated with those of the historian, who is usually less concerned than the anthropologist with the impact of well-known historic events upon the native population. What I propose to do, therefore, is to introduce members of the Berens family and other Indians as observers of or participants in historic events, as well as figures representative of certain aspects of the Indian culture of their period.

VOYAGE TO NORTHERN MANITOBA

The grub on the trail is strong black tea
And bacon by the yard
Now, let us boil a kettle and eat
"Bannock"* smeared with lard.

—A. I. Hallowell, field notes,
8 August 1930

*Bannock, in Manitoba, is a kind of flat quick bread easily fried over a campfire. Introduced by Scottish fur traders (the word is Scottish), it remains a standard native food.—Ed.

3

When, in the early summer of 1930, I boarded the little steamer *S. S. Keenora* at the city of Winnipeg, Manitoba, I had only the vaguest notions about the physiography and history of the region I was entering or the locations and ethnography of the Indian population. As we headed up Lake Winnipeg in the prolonged twilight, after following the tortuous windings of the Red River, my attention was focused on the Cree north of the lake. I was on my way to Norway House, about 300 miles north of Winnipeg, where there was a large reserve. I had given the Ojibwa peoples of the regions to the east and west of the lake little thought. Locally, they were known as Saulteaux. I soon found out that even in government documents as well as other writings, the differentiation between Cree and Saulteaux was sometimes badly confused, since no anthropologist had worked in this area.

It was not until I arrived at Norway House, on Little Playgreen Lake some 20 miles beyond the north end of Lake Winnipeg, that I began to appreciate the distinctive character of the Canadian wilderness. In particular, I was impressed by the survival of so many features from the past which, among both Indians and whites, were an integral part of the contemporary mode of life. Established in the early 19th century by the Hudson's Bay Company, Norway House was still functioning as an important trading post, although its heyday had passed. For it was long the divisional point through which all trade goods passed on their way from York Factory on Hudson Bay to posts in the far west and to the south. The renowned governor of the company, Sir George Simpson, once maintained a residence here, and it was at this post that the Council of the Northern Department of the company met annually and where the transfer of Rupert's Land to the Crown was arranged in 1869. Norway House was also a focal point of pioneer missionary activities in the 19th century. It was here that the Methodist James Evans (1801–1846) perfected an easily learned system of characters by means of which Indian languages could be written—his Cree syllabics.

Before the summer was over I ranged much farther into this northern wilderness. I made an 80-mile canoe trip to the Cross Lake Cree who had resisted Christianization for many years. On this reserve I saw a shaking tent performance for the first time, despite the fact that these Indians were nominally Christian. The conjurer made a prediction about some difficulties I would experience on the return trip, which proved to be true. I was also given eyewitness accounts by his sons of the miracles performed by a notorious "medicine man" of a previous generation, who had stoutly clung to his Indian world view. At the same time, I found myself only 50 miles east of the new railroad to Churchill on Hudson Bay, which had been opened the previous year after many delays and large expenditures. During the summer of my visit, the great grey cylinder of a terminal elevator, capable of storing 2 million bushels of grain, was erected at Churchill. But in the country through which I traveled, I saw nothing of this phase of contemporary civilization. On the contrary, I was struck by the stark, wild landscape, the silhouettes of endless stands of spruce on every horizon, the calm, dark lakes, the white rushing water of rapids, the innumerable portages, the muskeg, and the swarming mosquitoes, pests to Indians and white men alike.

The feel of the country itself became more deeply embedded in my experience by a trip to Island Lake, east of Norway House, where there was a reserve which was a composite of Cree and Ojibwa. This reserve was reached by a canoe route of some 160 miles, considered at the time to be one of the most arduous trips in that part of the country. At Island Lake I collected some genealogical material among the Ojibwa population relevant to clan membership and the marriage of cross cousins [see Chapter 4]; I also became aware that the Ojibwa were relatively recent arrivals in the region east of Lake Winnipeg. The realization of this historic fact brought me face to face with the problem of population movements in the Lake Winnipeg basin, which, instead of presenting questions that could be left to the archeologist, were events of the last two centuries, involved with the impact of the fur trade. Although I found these Indians to be much less acculturated in many respects than the Cree at Norway House and Cross Lake, to say nothing of the eastern Algonquian groups I had previously visited in the province of Quebec and along the shores of southern Labrador, it was evident that there were no strictly aboriginal peoples in this northern wilderness.

On the other hand, I was convinced that the presence of modern clothing, utensils, and ostensible Christianity were not reliable clues to their culture as a whole or when considered in psychological depth. There were retentions from the past that only detailed investigation could expose. It was evident that many complex variables had to be taken into account in order to understand the contemporary content and functioning of Indian culture. In addition to analysis, a historical perspective was inescapable. There were manifest cultural differences from group to group which, hypothetically, could only be explained by assuming the occurrence of differential rates of acculturation in response to varying historical events, such as the fur trade, movements of population, the local activities of missionaries, intermarriage with whites, and relations with the Dominion government.

My trip to Island Lake diverted my attention from the Cree to the Northern Ojibwa.[1] En route to the city of Winnipeg from the eastern United States, I had crossed Lake Huron by ship. I had passed through Sault Ste Marie and across Lake Superior to Port Arthur [Thunder Bay, Ontario] where I had changed to the railroad for the rest of my journey; the Sault, where in the summer months the whitefish were plentiful, was one of the ancient haunts of the Ojibwa. It was here, too, that Henry R. Schoolcraft, a pioneer American anthropologist, began his linguistic and ethnological inquiries among them when he went there as Indian agent in 1822 [Schoolcraft 1839]. Based upon the myths and tales collected by Schoolcraft, the Ojibwa of Lake Superior entered the American heritage with Longfellow's *The Song of Hiawatha* in 1855. Paul Kane painted an Ojibwa encampment near Sault Ste Marie in 1845 [Kane 1968 (1859):5], which was essentially like those I saw at Island Lake and later more than 100 miles up the Berens River.

In historical documents we first hear of the people later known as Ojibwa or Saulteaux in the *Jesuit Relations* of 1640 [Thwaites 1896–1901]. At this time they seem to have been confined to the country to the north of Lake Superior and along the Upper Peninsula of Michigan. Their early association with the Sault is the source of an Indian name for them—*People of the Falls or Rapids*—from which was derived the name given them by the French—*Saulteurs*. This name has persisted in anglicized form in parts of Canada down to the present time, alongside their alternative self-designation, *Anishinabek. Outchibouec* is an equally early designation which later took the English form *Ojibwa*. It is thought to have referred to the puckered seam of their moccasins [Rogers 1978:769]. *Chippewa* is actually a corrupted form of Ojibwa, but has received wide currency in the United States after having been officially adopted by the Bureau of American Ethnology. The Ojibwa today [1960s] constitute one of the largest Indian groups in the United States (32,000). In Canada, where they are found on more than 100 reserves in the provinces of Ontario, Manitoba, and Saskatchewan, they number close to 45,000. This wide geographical dispersion exemplifies at the same time an ethnohistorical problem.

Linguistically, the Ojibwa belong to the Central division of the once far-flung Algonquian stock. Speakers of this division once populated the region between Hudson Bay and the Ohio valley. North of the Great Lakes were the Cree (including the related Montagnais-Naskapi of the Labrador Peninsula) and the Ojibwa (including their close linguistic congeners, the Algonquin and Ottawa). South of the Great Lakes, in aboriginal times, the Central Algonquian languages were represented by the Menomini, Fox (with Sauk and Kickapoo), Miami, Illinois, Potawatomi, and Shawnee. The expansion of white settlements after the American Revolution, when the Appalachian barrier was finally breached, led to the displacement of the Central Algonquians south of the Great Lakes. By 1820, about one-third of the population of the United States was already to be found west of the Appalachian mountain range. Consequently, the Central Algonquian groups later investigated by anthropologists on reserves had undergone considerable social and cultural readjustment since aboriginal days. A broadly comparable situation transpired among the Cree, and particularly the Ojibwa, in Canada. But here radical changes occurred later, and external conditions permitted the conservation of older cultural forms in certain regions despite movements of population. In fact, it now appears that some of the northern representatives of the Central Algonquian linguistic groups may have retained the kinship terminology and the practice of cross-cousin marriage associated with it, which once characterized this entire group of peoples in aboriginal times [Hallowell 1928].

FIELDWORK WITH CHIEF WILLIAM BERENS

My interest in the Ojibwa of the Lake Winnipeg region was reinforced through the acquaintance I struck up early in the summer of 1930 with William Berens, who eventually became my interpreter, guide, and virtual collaborator in the investigations I carried on in subsequent years. I had gotten into conversation with him when the *S. S. Keenora* made its regular stop of an hour or so at the mouth of the Berens River. He was chief of the band which had a reserve there. This small river has its source about 300 miles to the southeast in Ontario and reaches Lake Winnipeg between 52 and 53 degrees north latitude. Its Indian name is Pigeon River *(omimisipi)*, referring to the long extinct passenger pigeon which was once found here in great migrating flocks and was a source of food. In the early 19th century the river began to appear on maps as *Berens*, being named after Joseph Berens, Jr., governor of the Hudson's Bay Company from 1812 to 1822 [Lytwyn 1986: 94n].[2] On modern maps, the next river to the south, which is shorter and parallels the Berens River, is named Pigeon River.

Figure 1. The S. S. Keenora *and the* Wolverine *docked at Berens River where Hallowell first met Chief Berens in July of 1930.*

Figure 2. Chief William Berens and his wife, Nancy Everett, about 1930–32, surrounded by family members. Clockwise from lower left: Ida May Berens, Alice (Dolly) Berens (Everett) with infant, Rosie Berens (married Antoine Bittern—see Fig. 4), Percy Berens, William Berens, Jr., Mary Rose (his wife), John Berens, and Bertha and Matilda Everett (Alice's daughters). Identifications courtesy of John and Maurice Berens, 1991.

7

At our first meeting I told Chief Berens that I would return for a visit later in the summer, and I did. It was on this second visit that, as a result of long conversations, my interest in the Ojibwa people east of Lake Winnipeg began to crystallize. From his account, it was clear that there had been much less acculturation inland than in the Cree and Ojibwa bands closer to the lake, including his own, and even compared with what I had seen for myself at Island Lake. I was particularly impressed by the fact that there were still un-Christianized Indians 250 miles up the river in the Pikangikum band. I knew of no other Algonquian group where this was the case. Besides this, Chief Berens said he would go with me if I wished to arrange a trip to Lake Pikangikum. He had not been this far inland since 1888 when, as a young man, he was a member of the party which surveyed the land for the Pikangikum reserve.

Two years later (1932) we made the trip to Lake Pikangikum together. In many respects it was an excursion into the living past. When I tried to engage Indian canoemen at the mouth of the river to make the trip, I ran into difficulty because practically none of the Indians in this locality had any knowledge whatever of the country to the east for more than 100 miles at most. Their phenomenal knowledge of the details of the terrain derived from direct knowledge and experience contrasted sharply with their ignorance of other parts of the country. Not accustomed to making use of a compass or modern maps, they remained at the aboriginal level of spatial orientation in traveling. Dependent upon familiar landmarks and local place names, and accustomed to moving from one known point of reference to another, any excursion into an unfamiliar region inevitably aroused considerable anxiety. The Berens River is not an easily traveled natural highway. There are tortuous windings of the river, many rapids, and cross-secting lakes; in the first 100 miles or so, 50 portages have to be made.

After we left what my friend Chief Berens called "civilization" at the mouth of the river, I also discovered that we had entered a more primitive world of temporal orientation. The days of the week melted away, as did the week as a unit of time, since no account was taken of the Sabbath. The naming of days of the week was concomitant with the spread of Christianity, on account of the significance given to the Sabbath. At the mouth of the river no one ever set out on a journey on Sunday, and church bells and school bells provided the effective signals that made it possible to assemble individuals at a given hour. As we ascended the river the hours of the day soon disappeared since I was the only person who carried a watch and it stopped. Consequently, we were all compelled to judge the time of day by the position of the sun. When we reached Lake Pikangikum, I discovered that one family had recently purchased an alarm clock. But hearing the alarm go off seemed more fascinating than the utility of the clock as a time-keeping device. In our trip up the river we *had* left some of the earmarks of western civilization behind. I became aware of the cultural gradient which existed at that time. Although even in William Berens' father's lifetime a common level of culture which embodied fur trade influences had prevailed, now the people at the mouth of the river had had their lives further transformed, so that relatively few traces of the earlier period remained. The farther inland I traveled, however, the more I found of the old ways surviving.

The inland Indians were still living in birchbark-covered dwellings and except for their clothing, utensils, and canvas canoes, one could easily imagine oneself in an encampment of a century or more before. Women were mending nets, chopping and hauling wood (among their most traditional tasks), and stitching the birchbark covers for their dwellings with spruce roots. They could be seen scraping and tanning skins for making moccasins, for this article of clothing was used by everyone, although rubbers, purchased from the trading post, might be worn over them. Babies were still snugly strapped to their cradleboards, being carried on these useful devices on their mothers' backs. Sphagnum moss, so intimately associated with them because the Indians had discovered its highly absorbent and deodorant properties, could be seen drying in the sun in almost every camp. Evidence of the importance of fish at this season was everywhere. Nets were in the water or being mended continually. One net I saw lifted in the middle of July at Lake Pikangikum comprised 30 whitefish, a dozen tullibees, several suckers, and a half dozen other fish of different varieties. Fish caught in the morning and scaled, gutted, and split lengthwise, could be seen being cured in the sun before being prepared for eating in the evening. Other fish were being lightly smoked on a rack for longer preservation. Berries were being picked by the women and children. As for the men, they were relatively idle but some, as at Island Lake, were to be seen making snowshoe frames or canoe paddles. There was frequent dancing on specially prepared ground, sometimes within a cagelike superstructure such as that used for the *Wabanowiwin,* although the Grand Medicine Lodge *(Midewiwin)* had died out. At night the beat of

Figure 3. Traveling on the Berens River with canoes and a "kicker" (a small outboard motor of 4–5 horsepower).

Figure 4. Joe Keeper, William Berens, A. I. Hallowell, and Antoine Bittern in 1935, probably at Little Grand Rapids. Photographer not identified. Antoine Bittern gave this picture to Stephen T. Boggs in the summer of 1952 when Boggs was a graduate student doing fieldwork at Berens River. Keeper and Bittern guided and cooked respectively when Hallowell traveled up the river. Information courtesy of John and Maurice Berens, 1991.

a water-drum often reverberated in one's ears. And, when some serious problem demanded the help of other than human persons, the shaking tent swayed after nightfall as the moon rose behind the tall dark spruces. From this enclosed structure, occupied by a conjurer, the voices of other than human beings spoke directly to the group of men, women, and children who encircled it [Hallowell 1942].

Although it is true that aboriginal culture as a fully rounded and comprehensive scheme of life had disappeared, a continuity with the past was obvious, along with a persistence of attitudes, values, beliefs, and behavior which had their roots in an aboriginal sociocultural system. This interpretation was thrown into sharper relief when I returned to the mouth of the river. Here no one ever beat a native drum. The shaking tent was never to be seen. The only dances to be observed were square dances. Those Ojibwa had long become accustomed to living in log cabins all the year round. No birchbark-covered dwellings were to be seen. Here everyone knew what day of the week it was and went to church on the Sabbath. And during the summer months, the weekly visits of the *S. S. Keenora* kept these Indians in direct touch with the outside world.

HISTORY THROUGH THE BERENS FAMILY

I have always considered it extremely fortunate that I met William Berens when I did. I soon discovered, as a consequence of the extensive genealogical inquiries that I initiated, that he and his forebears for three generations epitomized, as I have said, the broader sweep of historical events in the Lake Winnipeg area and the consequences of the acculturation process. In part, this was due to the fact that the Berenses were not an inland family and William Berens' mother, Mary McKay, was a white woman.[3] His ancestors on both sides had long been close to events on the local frontier. On his father's side there was a long conservative Indian tradition of which he was thoroughly cognizant; on his mother's side we find her lineal ancestors and relatives closely associated with the Hudson's Bay Company and the Métis of the Red River settlement.[4] On account of his father's choice of a wife, William Berens himself was bilingual from childhood and as fully acquainted with the ways of white men as Indians. Thus, from the beginning of my association with him, I became historically oriented as a matter of course because we made constant reference to the persons of past generations in the genealogical material we had collected together. This enabled me to integrate data concerning the cultural present with changes in the historic past, often with reference to specific individuals and to events external to the Berens River region, which could be checked in written documents.

Yellow Legs, the paternal great-grandfather of William Berens, must have been born around the middle of the 18th century and died not later than 1830. If so, the beginning of his life span was only about a generation subsequent to the time when the first white men of whom we have incontrovertible knowledge reached Lake Winnipeg from the east by way of the Winnipeg River. These were Frenchmen under the leadership of Pierre Gaultier de Varennes, Sieur de la Vérendrye. Descending the river they found the Cree on the right bank and on the left, the Assiniboine, a people speaking a Siouan language closely related to the Yankton Dakota. The same people were met at the forks of the Red and Assiniboine rivers, south of Lake Winnipeg, which La Vérendrye's party reached in 1738. The fact that they met no Ojibwa at this time is well supported by archeological as well as historical evidence [Steinbring 1980:124–128].

Yellow Legs may be considered then, to represent an Ojibwa of a later period after these people had started to move west of the Great Lakes and even beyond Lake Winnipeg because Yellow Legs was born on the west side of this lake.[5] It is also known that he was a leader of the Midewiwin, a ceremonial organization concerned with curing, which, even if not completely aboriginal in origin, embodied essential aspects of an aboriginal world view [on its debated origins, see Hickerson 1988:59–63, 142–143]. Many anecdotes survive of the miracles Yellow Legs performed. One of his great-grandsons, who was born before the wife of Yellow Legs died, told me that the old *mide* priest was once seen walking on the water over to a little island in Lake Winnipeg several miles east of the mouth of the Jack Head River. He was on his way to secure a special kind of "medicine." He was brought back by *memengwéciwak,* semihuman mythological creatures who live in the rocks and travel in canoes. The inference was that he obtained the medicine from them. He was a *manäo,* a type of curer who obtained his medicine from this source. All this happened in broad daylight while many people were watching. He also brought back some gulls' eggs from the island, "in order to make people believe in his power," my informant said.

On another occasion Yellow Legs dreamed of a large round stone on Egg Island, near the one already mentioned. He sent two men to fetch this stone for him. They were told to follow a bear's tracks to be found on the edge of the shore, which would lead them directly to it. To make sure they had found the right stone, they were told that a few branches would be broken directly above it. This stone was brought back and it later appeared in the Midewiwin lodge. It exhibited animate properties when Yellow Legs tapped it with a knife. A mouth, suggested by the external characteristics of the surface, would open and he would extract a packet of medicine. The medicine would be made into a concoction which was then shared by all present.

These anecdotes exemplify the traditional Ojibwa world view, which I shall discuss later on the basis of information collected in this century. They are thoroughly intelligible in terms of its premises. The famous stone of Yellow Legs finally reached the Berens River where his son Bear went to live. Bear, in cooperation with his brother, *Cauwanäs* (the One who travels with the South Wind), carried on the Midewiwin at the mouth of the river where William Berens saw the last performance as a child. The stone came into his possession and he never would part with it, although it no longer manifested any animate properties. It is interesting, too, that William once dreamed of the *memengwéciwak,* as his great-grandfather had. He said he could have obtained medicine from them but never did so.

Among the inland Ojibwa of the Berens River, the Midewiwin persisted into the 1920s. I was able to obtain a collection of a dozen bark scrolls with their characteristic pictographs, and other objects which are now in the Museum of the American Indian (Heye Foundation) in New York City. Morning Star, the last leader of the Midewiwin in the whole Lake Winnipeg basin, whom I visited in 1931, died the following year at Hollow Water River. The Midewiwin exemplifies the persistence of a ceremony, based on the traditional world view of the Ojibwa, which continued to flourish despite the impact of the fur trade, Christianization, and other acculturative influences. With its passing, some of the Midewiwin's functions were absorbed by the *Wabanowiwin.*

Bear (c. 1790–1871),[6] the oldest son of Yellow Legs, clung to the old Ojibwa world view like his father. He never was converted to Christianity. His younger brother *Cauwanäs,* however, although once associated with his father and brother in the Midewiwin, did become converted in later life. He was baptized Roderick Ross. It was during the generation of these men that the missionaries became active and Christian names and surnames derived from various sources began to be more widely adopted by the Indians. In the aboriginal system of nomenclature, each child was given a personal name in a Naming Feast held not long after birth. This custom continued long after the system of surnames and Christian names came into vogue. In the native system, a personal name was derived from a dream of the namer—an old man in the "grandfather" category. With the name were transferred "blessings" which the namer had received from other than human persons. Consequently, a personal name had a sacred quality and was seldom used in daily life. In this context, nicknames and kinship terms were sufficient for personal identification. But as increasing social interaction with whites occurred, a naming system derived from the culture of the white man began to function in interaction with non-Indians [cf. Rogers and Rogers 1978].

Bear was the first to take the surname Berens,[7] despite the fact that his brother, Cauwanäs, had adopted the surname Ross. In the next generation, however, one of the sons of Cauwanäs continued this surname [Ross], but one of his brothers became Felix and another took the surname MacDonald. These names of Indian families, appearing from this time on in the books of the Hudson's Bay Company and in church records, may seem confusing to the outsider. Actually, the process had its analogue only two or three centuries before in the history of surnames in Europe. Once adopted, the usage of surnames by the Ojibwa was easily reconciled with the patrilineal principle already well established in their culture by clan membership. Every Indian knew the personal names of all the men referred to here and could also address them or refer to them by kinship terms; everyone was also cognizant of the fact that all these men were descendants of Yellow Legs and belonged to the Moose clan. The adoption of patronymics for subdivisions within this clan had no functional significance in the Ojibwa sociocultural system.

Jacob Berens (c. 1829–1917), the father of William, maintained the surname his father, Bear, had adopted. He became an Indian of the "new order"; he did not cling to the past. His life history epitomizes the cumulative social and cultural changes that were deeply penetrating the old Indian way of life everywhere. Although there was no local missionary when he was a boy, he became a Christian nonetheless and was baptized in 1861 by the Methodist missionary at Norway House. He was active in bringing a resident missionary, Egerton R. Young, to Berens River in 1873. Although he hunted and fished like other Indians, he also worked for the Hudson's Bay Company a great deal of the time and, unlike his brothers, learned to speak English through this association with whites. And, instead of marrying an Indian girl, he chose a white woman, Mary MacKaye [McKay] as his wife. Her father, William, was born in Scotland and came to Canada in 1818.[8] Later he became manager of the Hudson's Bay Company post at the mouth of the river. In 1848, he established an outpost up the river on Family Lake, later the locale of the reserve of the Little Grand Rapids Band.

In the home of Jacob Berens both English and Ojibwa were spoken. William MacKaye lived with them, and Mary and her father always spoke in English. On the other hand, Jacob and his wife ordinarily used Ojibwa. William Berens told me that his mother always spoke to him in English from as far back as he could remember. "As soon as I started to go around and play with the Indian boys," he said, however, "I forgot all my English. When I was older and went working among white men I picked it up again because they spoke no Ojibwa" [Berens 1940]. When the Lake Winnipeg Treaty 5 was negotiated by the Dominion government in 1875, Jacob Berens signed it and became the first "chief" of the Indians of the Berens River region.

Since William Berens was born about 1865 he was in his middle sixties when I first met him. The pattern of his life history [cf. Brown 1989] may be considered to be a continuation of that of his father in a period when the changes initiated in the previous generation had become further accelerated and more deeply entrenched. Yet ties with the Indian past remained. Because of his paternal ancestry and boyhood experiences, he was thoroughly familiar with traditional Ojibwa culture. His association with me seemed to revivify his interest in it as a way of life. Everything that we saw on our trip to Lake Pikangikum was part of a living past for him because it was the kind of life he once had led. Like the Indians in these inland bands, he too had seen the Midewiwin, only at a much earlier period than they had. As a child he remembered his grandfather in the Midewiwin when it was last given at the mouth of the Berens River just before the latter's death. "I can't forget I had a small piece of dog meat passed to me and I ate it," he said. On the other hand, from childhood he was raised as a member of a Christian household. Like his father he worked from time to time for the Hudson's Bay Company. From early manhood, he also worked closely with white men in other jobs. In 1886, when F. W. Wilkins, employed by the Department of the Interior, made a micrometer survey of the shore of Lake Winnipeg, William was employed to carry the "target," and two years later, as I have said, he was a member of the party which surveyed the land for the reserve at Lake Pikangikum. The life histories of William Berens and his father exemplify the personal integration of the two cultural systems, which ever since the intrusion of Europeans into North America and the beginning of the fur trade had involved the Indians in a slow but continuing process of cultural readaptation and personal readjustment.

To appreciate this process and to understand the functioning of the sociocultural system of the Berens River Indians in the early decades of this century, it is necessary to widen our geographic and historical perspective because these Indians were both directly and indirectly affected by a very complex sequence of national and provincial events prior to this period. The links between these events and cultural continuity and change among the Berens River Indians will be briefly described in the next two chapters.

EDITOR'S NOTES

1. Hallowell's use of "Northern Ojibwa" diverges from more recent standard usage. The *Handbook of North American Indians,* vol. 6, *Subarctic* (Helm, ed. 1981) reserves the term for the people of interior northwestern Ontario from the upper tributaries of the Albany and Severn rivers to Island Lake, across the provincial border in Manitoba. Thus, Hallowell's "Northern Ojibwa" are classified among the "Lake Winnipeg Saulteaux," comprising the people of the southern and central Lake Winnipeg drainage from Lac Seul and Lake of the Woods, Ontario to Roseau River and Fisher River, Manitoba (see maps in Helm, ed. 1981:232, 245). The *Handbook* distinction appropriately takes account of some broad differences between these regions in dialect, historical ties, culture, and social organization. The Saulteaux had the Midewiwin, or Grand Medicine Society, and patrilineal clans; the Northern Ojibwa did not. *Saulteaux* is a customary self-designation among the Ojibwa people of Berens River and Lake Winnipeg, although *Ojibwa* and *Anishinabe* are preferred in some circles (Rogers and Taylor 1981:231; Steinbring 1981:244).

2. The river's carrying of two names, one Ojibwa and one European, is a consequence of the white men's habit of (re)naming geographical features that already had names. The naming of features after noted persons is a distinctly European custom; Algonquian names usually refer to important local traits of a site, or to some remembered event that occurred there.

William Berens' grandfather, Bear *(Mahquah),* passed down a Saulteaux version of how the river got its European name. A "Commissioner" of the HBC (probably Henry Hulse Berens who would have stopped at Berens River in September 1832 on his way from Norway House to Red River) noticed that strips of beaver skins cut up for tying bales of furs were lying around unused, and saw their value as decorative trimmings. As William Berens told Hallowell, the official "offered to give his name in exchange" to Bear. Bear replied, "Your name is no good to me—give it to the river—it may be some good to the Indians then since they can drink the water" ("a crack at the Company," as Hallowell noted) (Hallowell papers, Research, Saulteaux Indians). Bear kept his own name, but may have retained the idea of using Berens for the next generation. He probably knew that the Europeans were already calling the river "Berens"; possibly he was making an ironic comment on the fact that the river already bore the visitor's family name.

3. The Berens River people would have viewed Mary McKay Berens as white on the basis of cultural attributes such as her use of English, her patrilineal ancestry going back to Scotland, her membership in an established fur trade company family, and possibly her appearance. Both her parents, however, were of mixed Algonquian–European descent. She was one of thousands of offspring of families formed by European traders and native women in the period before white settlement began to spread into the Canadian northwest (Brown 1980, Van Kirk 1980).

4. Separate terms for people of mixed race (such as *Métis,* from a French word meaning "mixed," or "halfbreed") were not in use in Berens River, or indeed in the old HBC trading regions extending from Hudson and James bays to Lake Winnipeg. These categories spread westward to Red River with the Montreal-based Canadian fur trade, having arisen in older colonial contexts where such distinctions became important. For comparative perspectives, see Peterson and Brown, eds. 1985.

5. Berens family members have disputed this point, believing Yellow Legs came from the east, although in his later life he and his kin certainly had ties to and were familiar with the region west of Lake Winnipeg.

6. The last reference to Bear in the Hudson's Bay Company post records at Berens River appears to be in October of 1873, and he may have been the "old Indian" who was buried there on 13 February 1874 (Hudson's Bay Company Archives, Provincial Archives of Manitoba [HBCA,PAM] B.16/a/7, fo. 27).

7. In contemporary HBC and church records, the first Saulteaux to use the name Berens was Jacob, the son of Bear. In Jacob's baptismal record at Norway House, dated 25 February 1861, his father was named as *Mahquah,* the Saulteaux word for bear (Methodist baptismal register, no. 1110). This usage is consistent with Bear's rejection of the name Berens, as recounted in note 2. Bear may ultimately have encouraged Jacob to elect that surname, which not only came from an important official but also sounded something like Bear and designated the family's home.

8. William McKay indeed spent several years in Scotland with his father, Donald McKay (or MacKay), who had served first in the Montreal-based fur trade and later in the Hudson's Bay Company. William was, however, not Scottish-born but, as Governor George Simpson noted in his employees' "Character Book" of 1832, "a halfbreed of the Cree nation" (Williams, ed, 1975:234). His mother was a native-born daughter of HBC inland trader James Sutherland (d. 1797) and his fur trade wife, who was probably Cree. Donald married Sutherland's daughter "according to the custom of the country," as the traders phrased it (cf. Brown 1980). After her death he brought William and another son to his home parish of Clyne, Sutherlandshire, where the boys were presumably educated (Duckworth 1988:40, 42). William left Scotland in 1817 to start his HBC career (HBCA, PAM, B, 239/ d/195, fo. 9d–10a).

The Berens River people were not "wrong" when they classed William as Scottish (or his daughter as white); see notes 3 and 4, above. Both Algonquian peoples and old HBC men assigned ethnic identity on the basis of one's principal social, cultural, and economic affiliations rather than by the European folk categories of "race" or "blood," which became pervasive in the 19th century.

2 / The Canadian Shield, The Fur Trade, and Ojibwa Expansion

GEOGRAPHY AND FURS

Lake Winnipeg lies on the western edge of the great Canadian Shield, the dominant physiographic feature which underlies 65 percent of the Dominion. The Shield is geologically characterized by the outcrop of more than 2 million square miles of Precambrian crystalline granite, the oldest rocks on this continent. It surrounds Hudson Bay in an arc extending to the Mackenzie basin in the northwest, south to the Great Lakes, and east to Labrador. Following the northern shores of the Great Lakes it skirts the eastern margins of the lower Red River Valley and Lake Winnipeg. To the west of this body of water, we enter a different physiographic region, the great Central Plains of North America.

The Canadian Shield was intensely glaciated until perhaps 4500 B.C. By late postglacial times the great coniferous forest of the subarctic boreal zone became its characteristic cover. Spruce, balsam, fir, jack pine, and birch are dominant; poplar, willow, and alder are frequent. It was this region that became the habitat of the moose, the woodland caribou, the black bear, deer, and wolverine and such fur-bearing animals as the beaver, marten, mink, fisher, otter, lynx, muskrat, and fox. In the eastern subarctic, the region with which we are chiefly concerned here, the country is laced with an intricate system of lakes and rivers whose waters teem with edible fish: whitefish, sturgeon, trout, pike, pickerel, and perch. More than 300 species of birds have been reported, as migrants or residents. But on the land, muskeg (from the Cree word for swamp) and sterile soils prevail for the most part. It is a region basically unfitted for agriculture. For a long time it was a physical barrier to the national development and unification of Canada.

On the other hand, the Canadian Shield, once the great ice sheets had receded, became populated by native peoples whose economy was based on hunting and fishing. When the Indians who later became known as Saulteaux, Ojibwa, or Chippewa, entered the historical picture, the portion of the Canadian Shield north of Lake Superior already was their habitat, a fact now supported by archeological evidence. Alfred Kroeber [1939] pointed out many years ago that in the eastern subarctic, this physiographic formation coincided quite well with the distribution of the Algonquin–Ottawa–Ojibwa in the Great Lakes area, the Cree inhabiting the region bordering immediately on Hudson Bay.[1]

Beginning with the 17th century the Canadian Shield, precisely because of the fauna which characterized it, became the heartland of one of the greatest business enterprises of the past—the fur trade. It included that vaguely defined territory which became famous as Rupert's Land when, by charter from the British Crown in 1670, it became, in effect, the sovereign territory of the Hudson's Bay Company. As yet unexplored, the Shield was originally defined as the region whose waters flowed into Hudson Bay and Strait. As a matter of geographical fact, when the country did become known, the Hudson Bay depression at the heart of the Shield was found to drain about half the Canadian mainland through the Nelson–Saskatchewan River system, and through the Churchill, Severn, Albany, and other rivers which flow into Hudson Bay.

Therefore, stimulated by the competition for furs, La Verendrye's (and associates') solution in the 18th century of the puzzle presented by the waterways of the Lake Winnipeg basin represented a major discovery. For Lake Winnipeg was not explored at an early period, although it proved to be pivotal to later explorations. Although tiny compared with its glacial ancestor, gigantic Lake Agassiz, which was as large as the three upper Great Lakes combined, Lake Winnipeg ranks fifth in size among the inland waters of the continent. It is 260 miles long and 65 miles across at its widest point. It receives the Saskatchewan River at its northwest corner, thus being fed with waters from the far-off Rocky Mountain Divide, and providing a direct artery to the far west. On the south the Red River empties into Lake Winnipeg, and, at its southeast corner, the Winnipeg River brings waters from the height of land near Lake Superior. At the same time, Lake Winnipeg discharges its own waters through the turbulent Nelson River, which emerges from its northern end and leads to Hudson Bay. On the other hand, the small rivers flowing into the eastern side of Lake Winnipeg, such as the Berens, Poplar, Bloodvein, and so on, drain a height of land between the lake and the Bay and lead nowhere.[2]

During the height of the old fur trade period, Lake Winnipeg became the crossroads of a continent. Trade routes from the east as well as from Hudson Bay cut through it, since the traders from Montreal developed canoe routes across the Great Lakes which also led them to Lake Winnipeg and the Saskatchewan River. Once the basic pattern of the waterways of the Lake Winnipeg basin became known to white men, trade goods eventually reached the Indians everywhere in Rupert's Land and initiated processes of acculturation and other events which rapidly affected the lives of people who, up to this time, had only the relatively meagre technological equipment of a stone age culture.

The Ojibwa, like other Indians of the upper Great Lakes before they were discovered by Europeans, probably had their cultural roots in some regional variation of the Late Woodland period (A.D. 800–1600), which archeologists have been bringing into sharper focus in recent years. Although it is unnecessary to go into detail here, the technological changes, the redistribution of the aboriginal population, and intergroup influences which occurred during the fur trade period can scarcely be overemphasized in terms of their cultural consequences. It should not be forgotten that all later ethnographic descriptions were made subsequent to these changes. The Ojibwa are only a specific example of processes and events that were occurring over a wide area [Harris and Matthews 1987, plates 38–40]. Iron needles, awls, files, knives, scissors, axes, kettles, woven cloth, and thread were among the standard articles being made available to the Indians by the Hudson's Bay Company by the middle of the 18th century, to say nothing of firearms, beads, pigments, mirrors, and alcohol.

The Ojibwa had previously depended upon stone and bone tools; they used bowls and spoons made of wood, out of which they also shaped the frames of their snowshoes, drums, sleds, cradleboards, and paddles for their canoes. The latter were made of birchbark. In form they are a familiar image to us because the Ojibwa type of canoe has provided us with the stereotype of the Indian canoe. From prehistoric times, these people also manufactured containers of bark. Sewn together into oblong pieces with split spruce roots, rolls of the bark of the white birch were long and easily transportable and covered the framework of three or four poles that they used for the skeleton of their dwellings. Cattail mats might be used, too. The Ojibwa spun twine from nettle fiber and wove bags of bark twine. Clothing for the upper part of the body as well as leggins and moccasins were made of skin, tanned by the women, and sewn with sinew. And in winter the skins of the varying hare, easily snared, were cut into strips and looped into a fabric by a knotless netting technique. For hunting, the Ojibwa were dependent on the spear and the bow and arrow; for trapping animals, on deadfalls. Nets and weirs were made for catching fish, second only to game as a stable article of diet. Composite fishhooks were available, and spearing was practiced. Some basketry was known, as was simple cord-decorated pottery, possibly in several varieties.

For people with a material culture of such a limited range and involving only elementary techniques, the practical consequences of the newly acquired trade objects upon their daily lives and aboriginal ecological adaptation were tremendous. Methods of hunting were transformed, some old handicrafts like pottery making quickly became obsolete when kettles became available, and since the traders provided a wider and wider range of goods as time went on, processes of cultural change in the material sphere have continued down to the present. At the same time, it should not be forgotten that the continuing demand for furs, in the long run, entrenched most of these Indians more firmly in their occupation as hunters since so many of them were compelled to remain in a region where any transition to agriculture was impossible.

The commercial transactions developed with the traders placed the Indians in a novel position through the system of "debt" which was foreign to their own economic organization. It was necessary for the traders to furnish Indian hunters with goods on credit, trusting them to bring in fur in payment after they had made their catch. The risk became even greater when competing companies or free traders all offered credit. Consequently, high prices were charged for the goods sold to the Indians and, since there were cyclic fluctuations in the abundance of fur-bearing animals from natural causes, as well as differential skills and other variables, it was difficult for the Indians to keep out of "debt." They became increasingly dependent upon trade goods, yet it was impossible for them to borrow and learn metallurgical or other techniques, so wholly foreign to their stone age cultural background. They could not revolutionize their own technological culture to learn to manufacture the trade articles so avidly desired and raise their standard of living to a new level through economic independence. Although guns, for example, were acquired

Figure 5. Making a rabbit-skin blanket.

Figure 6. Stretching a hide. People of the Poplar Hill (Ont.) area have identified these women as Helen (Mrs. Stanley) Quill and her aunt, Ohkanchiish, daughter of Sakashki (courtesy of Gary Butikofer).

by the middle of the 18th century, when these weapons needed repair it was necessary to take them to the blacksmith at a trading post, or purchase new ones. It was only possible for the northern Indians to obtain the goods they wanted by becoming parties to commercial transactions that involved them in an economic system external to their native culture and provincial mode of life. At this level they had to remain hunters and fishermen. This was a limiting and conservative factor with respect to the range and character of possible changes in other aspects of their sociocultural systems.[3]

THE EXPANSION OF THE OJIBWA

The impact of the fur trade upon the northern Indians, as I have said, involved more than the acquisition of new types of tools, clothing, utensils, firearms, and food-stuffs. The Ojibwa are an example of an ethnic group which expanded their range tremendously both through warfare and peaceful movements. Some of them appear to have identified themselves more completely with the white fur traders than other Indians, so that their livelihood as well as their population movements became linked with the vicissitudes of the fur trade. This very complex historical picture has not been fully documented or described and analyzed in detail. We cannot de-termine from historical sources alone how unified Ojibwa culture was prior to the 17th century, but archeological investigations now in progress may provide relevant information. What we do know is that broad regional differences in social and cultural readjustments are of primary importance in later periods. Consequently, it has become more and more hazardous, or even impossible, to generalize about the Ojibwa as a whole. Here it will only be necessary to present the bare historical facts in outline, with emphasis on the Northern Ojibwa. This division of these people remained within the Canadian Shield, in the eastern subarctic, which is likewise the region in which the Berens River Indians are found. As for the southeastern division of the Ojibwa, in the 18th century they moved into the lower peninsula of Michigan and eastern Ontario, where some of them remained hunters and fishermen and others became farmers [Tanner 1987: map 13].

Chronologically, the period between 1700 and 1800 marked the peak of Ojibwa expansion in almost every direction. But other ethnic groups had been shifting their positions too, which is what makes both the historic and prehistoric picture so complex. Although the Cree surrounded the lower portion of Hudson Bay in the 17th century, it now seems probable that they had penetrated much farther to the south at a much earlier period than was once thought. Archeological evidence, for example, covering the era from 3000 B.C. to A.D. 1750 in southeastern Manitoba, shows six successive and distinguishable foci. The earliest indicate relationships with the northern Great Plains. The Manitoba focus seems to represent the presence of the Assiniboine (A.D. 1000–1250). However, the Selkirk focus which follows it (1350–1750) has been interpreted as representing the prehistoric and early historic remains of the Cree, who were probably intruders from the north or northeast into an area previously occupied by Siouan-speaking people. In any case, there are no archeological remains that suggest the presence of Ojibwa, and when Alexander

Henry the Elder reached the mouth of the Winnipeg River in 1775, he found a Cree settlement there [Henry 1969:245–246]. At this time the Assiniboine were on the prairie south and west of Lake Winnipeg adjoining the country of their linguistic congeners, the Sioux.[4]

In the 18th century, some Ojibwa were moving west of Fond du Lac (the western end of Lake Superior) into the headwaters of the Mississippi River where they came into possession of part of the country formerly occupied by Siouan-speaking peoples. This movement defines the region later occupied by the *South-western Ojibwa,* discussed by Harold Hickerson [1962]. This branch of the Ojibwa not only left the environmental area of the Canadian Shield, but the subarctic zone, and was soon plunged into many intensified contacts with whites. By the end of the 18th century (1794) a few Ojibwa already were residing west of Lake Winnipeg, although still within the subarctic region. This branch later became known as the *Plains Ojibwa* since some of them moved farther south, became bison hunters, and were influenced by other aspects of the culture of the Indians of the northern Plains [Howard 1977].

In the lower Red River Valley, southwest of the Canadian Shield, the Ojibwa had become well established by the early 19th century. Here they were called Saulteaux, referring to their former association with Sault Ste Marie, or *Bungi,* meaning "a little of something," because of their reputed habit of asking the settlers for a little of this or that.[5] They joined the whites in the bison hunting that was carried on from this locality. It was in the Red River Valley, too, that considerable race mixture took place, leading to the emergence of the *Métis*. This group became dominant in the Red River Colony for a long period and, differentiating themselves from both Indians and whites, attempted to achieve a measure of political independence through setting up a provisional government in 1869–1870.[6]

When Lord Selkirk found it desirable to make a treaty with the Indians of the Red River in 1817, five years after he had established the first settlers there, it is significant that although both Cree and Ojibwa were included, it was Peguis, an Ojibwa Indian, with whom he carried on negotiations, although the Ojibwa were intruders in this region. Peguis was very friendly with the settlers and under his leadership the Ojibwa became more influential than ever before. The treaty he helped to promote was, moreover, the first to be negotiated between a British subject and the Indians of Rupert's Land. It paved the way for the acquisition by the Dominion of Canada of the whole of the northwest, half a century later.

Another spur of Ojibwa expansion from the Lake Superior borderland led to the deeper penetration of the country farther north and the occupation of the region directly east of Lake Winnipeg. In contrast with the western movements already referred to, this one led deeper into the subarctic zone and into a physical environment not radically different from the Ojibwa habitat of prehistoric times. It was somewhat less rich in deciduous trees, but, except in a very technical sense, the biota and topography were essentially the same since it still lay within the borders of the Shield. Furthermore, no people of basically different native culture were met, and the region was farther from the main avenues of the fur trade. Temporally, this movement paralleled the one which ultimately reached the prairies, or possibly occurred a little later. There is some documentary evidence that Ojibwa groups were already occupying this northern region prior to the last quarter of the 18th century [Lytwyn 1986:18, 27]. So we may picture the Northern Ojibwa at this time in possession of an aboriginal culture only modified by the articles available to them in the 18th century fur trade. Missionary influences certainly had not begun as yet.

The next stage in acculturative influences, as was the case with the Berens River Ojibwa, was chiefly mediated through more intensive direct contacts with local trading posts and resident missionaries. Yet the region east of Lake Winnipeg long remained isolated from other white influence in the 19th century, not only because of its inhospitable nature, but because it fell within the area still dominated by the Hudson's Bay Company until the political birth of the Dominion of Canada in 1867. Except for the impact of the fur trade, the new setting in which the Northern Ojibwa found themselves was one which permitted cultural changes of an ecologically adaptive character. At the same time, it was possible for some cultural continuities from the aboriginal past to be preserved.

GENEALOGICAL EVIDENCE

When I analyzed the genealogies of the Ojibwa of the Berens River, collected in the early 1930s from the oldest men and women then living on the river from its mouth to Lake Pikangikum, I found that this material dovetailed perfectly with the historical and archeological evidence. The progenitors of every patrilineal line that I recorded originally came to the Berens River from some locality outside. In many lines my genealogies covered individuals of five generations. Yellow Legs, for example, the great-grandfather of William Berens, belonged to what I have designated "Generation II" in the correlation of my data. The birth dates of all individuals of Generations I and II fall in the 18th century. Those of "Generation V," like William Berens, link individuals of the 19th century with the 20th. I failed to discover a single white ancestor in the genealogies of the inland Indians of the Berens River. On the other hand, there were several intermarriages between Indians and whites in the ancestry of the Indians at the mouth of the river. These Ojibwa had been close to major trade routes and trading posts and in other ways had come into more direct contacts with the white population since the 18th century.

The fact that the Ojibwa have a system of patrilineal clans, with mammal, fish, and bird names, simplified the ordering of the genealogical data. I discovered, moreover, that a clan might consist of more than one lineage and that the progenitors of different lineages of the same clan reached the Berens River from different directions. There was direct evidence, besides, that lineages representing different clans had moved into the Berens River region from all directions except the north. The Moose clan, for example, was found to include two lineages. One of these, which included the Berens family and other Moose at the mouth of the river, stemmed from Yellow Legs. Since he reached the Berens River from the west side of Lake Winnipeg, his ancestors must have been among the Ojibwa who later became known as the Plains Ojibwa. The members of the other lineage of the Moose clan were only found inland, 150 miles and more up the Berens River. This lineage came from the Lac Seul district (Ontario) to the southeast. The oldest man

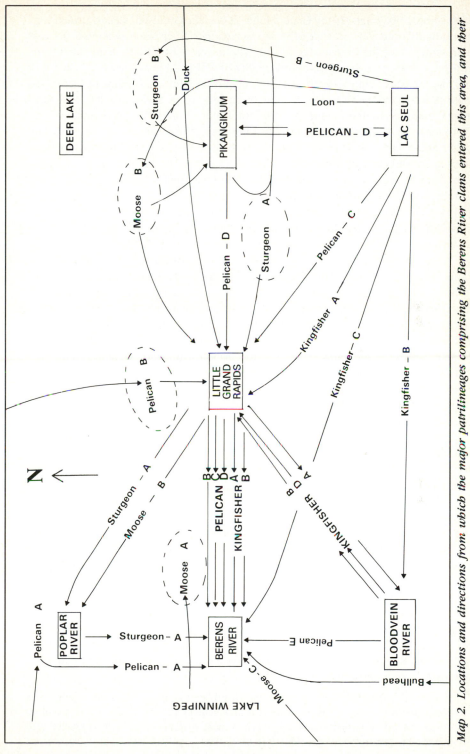

Map 2. Locations and directions from which the major patrilineages comprising the Berens River clans entered this area, and their subsequent movements from the late 1700s to the 1930s. Map redrawn from original in A. I. Hallowell papers, American Philosophical Society, Philadelphia.

of this lineage belonged to my Generation I. It was his grandson, Cenawagwaskang, traditionally notorious because of his six wives and 20 children, who was the first representative of the Moose clan inland. The ancestry of all later members of this group converged on him [Hallowell 1938:249–250].

The Pelicans comprised a number of unconnected lineages. Some of them must have reached the eastern side of Lake Winnipeg from across the lake, whereas others came from the southeast. William Berens' paternal grandmother, Amo (Victoria), the wife of Bear, belonged to the lineage that came from the west. Her father belonged to an Ojibwa group on the Saskatchewan River near Cumberland House, the oldest post of the Hudson's Bay Company in the interior.[7] One of the two Sturgeon lineages came from the east, the other from Lac Seul. From this latter district, too, in addition to a Moose and a Sturgeon lineage, came two Kingfisher and two Pelican lineages, as well as the single lineage which constitutes the Loon clan. From an easterly direction came the Ducks, a single lineage, as were the Bullheads who migrated from the south to the mouth of the Berens River.

As might be expected in view of the expansion of the Ojibwa, the names of clans found on the Berens River, from the mouth to Lake Pikangikum, are reported in other localities outside this area where Ojibwa-speaking peoples are found. For the Ojibwa as a whole, at least three dozen animal names for clans have been recorded. Eight of these occur on the Berens River. In the 1930s their numerical frequency in the total population of the river was in descending order: Sturgeon, Moose, Pelican, Kingfisher, Loon, Duck, Caribou, Bullhead. Members of the first four clans constituted 82 percent of the Ojibwa population of the river at that time. The first five, moreover, were reported by Duncan Cameron from the Lake Nipigon region north of Lake Superior at the very beginning of the 19th century [Masson, ed., vol. 2, 1960:246].

These migrants to the region east of Lake Winnipeg seem to have been well established there by the early 19th century. Like other Northern Ojibwa they remained comparatively isolated in this enclave of the Shield. Bearing in mind that no roads or railroad lines have ever been built in this area, and no towns or cities have arisen, it becomes apparent why a native population with an economy based on hunting and fishing could persist relatively undisturbed. Even in the 20th century the population is less than five persons per square mile. Compared with the prairie regions to the west of Lake Winnipeg which, once they became accessible to settlement in the 19th century, proved so hospitable to agriculture, the building of roads and railroads, and the rise of towns and cities, this region within the Shield remained a backwater.

It is possible that the earliest *local* contacts of the Berens River Ojibwa with white traders date from the close of the 18th century, since there is oral tradition to this effect. It is said that these earliest traders represented the North West Company with whom the lineages inland may well have been in contact in the Lake Superior area before moving farther north.

It is traditional among the Indians that the North West Company traders not only had a post at the river mouth, but also at what is now called Old Fort Rapids, a distance of 40 miles up the river. Jim MacDonald, a man almost 90 years of age (1934) remembered hearing his great-grandmother (the wife of Yellow Legs) tell about an occurrence one winter when the NWC men at the former post were at the point of starving. The men came over to where she and her husband were camped. One of them said, "you look fat," and felt her arm. They gave Yellow Legs rum and some ammunition to kill a moose for them. After her husband killed the moose, she said, they moved their camp. They were frightened by the way these white men had acted [Hallowell 1935–1936:section 1, 7–8].[8]

However this may be, it is a matter of record that the Hudson's Bay Company built a post at the mouth of the river in 1814 [Lytwyn 1986:137]. The post was named for Joseph Berens, Deputy Governor of the company from 1807 to 1812 and Governor from 1812 to 1822. This was in the time of William Berens' grandfather Bear who, as I have pointed out, was the first to adopt Berens as a surname [but see Chapter 1, n.2]. This post has remained the focal trading establishment on the eastern side of Lake Winnipeg between Fort Alexander and Norway House.

In the early days of the fur trade it was a common practice for the master of a local post to make one or more of the best hunters a sort of unofficial agent. The man chosen was held more or less responsible for seeing to it that the other Indians brought in all their fur to the post. A similar custom was followed on the Berens River during most of the 19th century. The trading chief usually received a new suit of clothes every year, rum, tobacco, and a large red feather which he wore on his hat. These men were not invested with any institutionalized authority in the native system of social organization [but compare Francis and Morantz 1983:44–45]. But those whom I have identified in my genealogies all possessed power from other than human sources. They were famous as curers, conjurers, and leaders of the Midewiwin. At the mouth of the river Fair Wind, a Kingfisher somewhat older than William Berens' father was a trading chief. Up the river, Cenawagwaskang, already mentioned as the progenitor of the inland members of the Moose clan, played a similar role, and two men of the Pikangikum Band, who were the sons of trading chiefs and leaders of the still un-Christianized contingent of this band, were among my chief informants.[9]

TRADE GOODS, OLD AND NEW

As compared with the range of trade goods available in the early 18th century, many articles were added later in that century and as the 19th century wore on. Although tobacco was of New World origin it was not known to the northern Indians until introduced by the British and French after it had become widely known in Europe in the 17th century. Steel traps were a relatively late introduction. They only spread slowly around the beginning of the 19th century. Tea did not become a trade article until almost the second decade of the 18th century. But later, we not only find tea, but flour for making bannock, and pork, salt, and sugar. William Berens' great uncle, the younger brother of Bear, is said to have been the first Indian to drink tea in the Berens River band, and his maternal grandmother made her weekly cup a part of the Sabbath ritual. This habit became more common in his father's time, and ubiquitous in the 20th century. Even in William's boyhood, flour was still not generally used. Sturgeon caught in the spring as they ascended the rivers to spawn were sliced and smoked. "Then the dry sturgeon was pounded," he recalled. "The women would make birchbark rogans [containers] and fill them up. In the morning a woman would take a cupful of pounded sturgeon, dump it on a plate and mix sturgeon oil with it. That was a good breakfast for a man. There was no bread for the Indian then" [Berens 1940]. At this time no forks or plates were used. Matches became trade articles in the 19th century, displacing the flint and steel method for making fire, which long before had replaced aboriginal methods. At first, the company only doled them out to its own employees in cases where flint and steel failed.

By the end of the 19th century, however, articles of clothing such as men's pants, overalls, and underwear were available. In 1932, at a small branch post of the Hudson's Bay Company at Poplar Hill, 200 miles up the Berens River, in addition to such old standard articles as those already referred to, men's shirts and windbreakers, sweaters, rubbers (to be worn over moccasins), lard, woolen socks, candles, and soap were also to be found in the store. At larger posts the stock available was even wider in range, indicative of a market which had been continually expanding for more than two centuries. At the same time, the Indians at Poplar Hill in the 1930s typified the differential rate of acculturation that occurred among the Northern Ojibwa. For despite their dependence upon trade goods, which had been available to them through an outpost established in 1895, it was here and at nearby Duck Lake that the un-Christianized Indians of the Berens River were to be found. Compared with the changes that had been going on at the mouth of the river, the mode of life of these inland people remained remarkably conservative.

EDITOR'S NOTES

1. The best visual summaries of the glacial, environmental, and early human history of the Canadian Shield are plates 1, 4, and 6–9 of the *Historical Atlas of Canada* (Harris and Matthews 1987).

2. Victor Lytwyn (1986) has documented extensive fur trade activity across this region (the Petit Nord or Little North) to 1821. Rather than "nowhere," the rivers led to excellent furs and trade connections in that period.

3. See Francis and Morantz 1983, Thistle 1986, and Brown's and Peers' review essay in Hickerson 1988 for some discussions and sources on the complex, variable, and much-debated influences of the fur trade. The historical roles and relative utility of European firearms are also matters of debate (e.g., Townsend 1983).

4. For recent perspectives on the challenges of tracing native groups and their movements in these regions through archeological and ethnohistoric data, see Syms 1982 and Meyer 1987.

5. The Montreal traders generally used the term, *Saulteaux*, whereas *Bungi*, or *Bungee*, goes back to an 18th-century Hudson's Bay Company usage (Peers 1987:22–26).

6. Métis ethnic distinctiveness has been traced back to the 18th-century Great Lakes and the families formed by French fur traders and Northern Algonquian women. In 19th-century Red River, the people known as Métis were largely of francophone, Roman Catholic/Ojibwa-Cree background. Under Louis Riel, they formed a provisional government in 1869–1870, to resist Canada's effort to absorb Rupert's Land without offering means of consultation or representation to its inhabitants. For a recent summary and list of sources, see Brown 1987a.

7. In October of 1775, Alexander Henry the Elder had a memorable encounter with a chief, "Chatique, or The Pelican," at The Pas (Manitoba), downriver from Cumberland House (Henry 1969:259–261). Henry, as Katherine Pettipas has noted (1980:188), gave no ethnic identification for The Pelican; a more recent study (Thistle 1986:52–53) simply assumes he was Cree. Internal evidence from Henry's writings and the dynamics of the encounter itself, however, suggest he was more likely Ojibwa. The problems of identifying this elusive possible ancestor of the Berens family and of postulating a Pelican "clan" in the region, present in microcosm the challenges of interpretive ethnohistory. Some

scholars have noted the danger of "assuming all occurrences of animal group names . . . refer to totemic groups or clans"; the Ojibwa "Cranes" of northern Ontario, for example, go back to a man of that name and were not a totemic, unilineal, or exogamous clan (Rogers and Rogers 1982:168, 170).

8. In the late 1930s, Hallowell drafted some chapters and outlines for a book, *Pigeon River People*, that was never completed. Internal and external evidence (see Fewkes 1937) dates the text to around 1935–1936. The Nor'Wester's remark, "You look fat," in the passage quoted here would have suggested to the Ojibwas that these strangers might be incipient windigos (cannibalistic beings); see Henry 1969:200–201 for a close parallel.

9. In *Pigeon River People*, section I, p. 10, Hallowell adds that the Ojibwa used the term *ätawaganiogimakan*, "barter chief," to describe the trading chief position: William Berens "used the term, 'fur chief,' but *ätawagan* means 'anything given to a trader in exchange for his goods, especially fur or skins of wild animals [Baraga's Ojibwa dictionary] so that 'barter' seems to cover the meaning more exactly."

3 / Christianization, Confederation, and Treaties with the Indians

In addition to the influence of the fur trade upon the lives of the Indians, two other subsequent sources of more radical changes must be mentioned. These were (1) the activities of missionaries, intent upon changing the fundamental outlook and values of the Indians and (2) the federation of the older provinces and the creation of new ones, which brought the Dominion of Canada into being in 1867 and forced the Indians into the orbit of a modern political state.

THE MISSIONARIES

Although the Indians of this area had some sporadic contacts with missionaries in the 18th century, no effective Christianization occurred in the Lake Winnipeg region until long after the Red River Colony had been established in the early 19th century. Alexander Ross, the early historian of that settlement, writing of the period just prior to 1838 after visiting some Indian camps on the southern shores of Lake Winnipeg, says:

> In this quarter, idolatry and superstition reign unmolested. These children of nature, we may with truth say, have not to this hour heard, except at a distance, of revealed religion, nor the sound of the gospel, although living in the vicinity of the settlement. Neither Roman Catholic priest nor Protestant minister, though stationed in Red River for nearly twenty years, has ever visited these wretched beings at their camps. Could they draw nearer the settlement and find the means of living, they would no doubt be taken by the hand and receive instruction; but hitherto, with the exception of any advantage derived from the Hudson's Bay Company, they have remained a hopeless and friendless race [Ross 1972:206].

It was not long, however, before organized efforts to Christianize the natives of the Lake Winnipeg wilderness and of the area even farther west and northwest were initiated. From 1840 on, missionary activity began to expand. In this year the British Wesleyan Methodist Missionary Society selected Norway House in Cree country as the base of operations. James Evans was put in charge. Missionaries were also sent to Cumberland House and The Pas and later to Grand Rapids at the mouth of the Saskatchewan River. The Cree at Cross Lake, however, remained pagans for 30 years or more. In the same decade the Roman Catholic Oblate Fathers began to penetrate the country far to the northwest. However, as late as 1854, when the Reverend John Ryerson made an inspection tour, there were no missions of any kind on the eastern shores of Lake Winnipeg between Fort Alexander, near the mouth of the Winnipeg River and Norway House, far to the north. In fact, of a total of 18 Protestant missionaries in the Northwest at this time, six were in the Red River Colony.

When Ryerson stopped at the mouth of the Berens River en route to the north, he reported that the Indians themselves wished to have a local missionary [Ryerson 1855:125, 81]. Nothing seems to have been done in response until after Egerton R. Young, later a prolific writer of books about his pioneer experiences as a missionary, took over the Cree mission at Norway House in 1868. Here a delegation of Ojibwa from Berens River visited him. One of the leaders was Jacob Berens, who had previously visited Norway House, had learned the Cree syllabics, and had been baptized by the Reverend George McDougall, a missionary who began his tenure there in 1860.[1] In 1873, E. R. Young initiated the first mission at Berens River. He sent two converted Norway House Cree to hew logs and build a mission house [Young 1890:190–191, 252–254]. William Berens recalled seeing them at work, and Young recorded further details in one of his books [1890:258–262].

At this time there was a consensus among the missionaries that, compared with the Cree, the Ojibwa were extremely obdurate to conversion. Young evidently found them so because he referred to the "superstitious degradation" of the "little bands scattered along the eastern shores" of Lake Winnipeg and inland. As for the Berens River Ojibwa, he called them "a wicked and degraded tribe . . . so different from the more peaceful Crees." Nevertheless, his heart rejoiced that he had been given the opportunity of "seeing some golden sheaves gathered in for the heavenly garner" [1890:265]. By 1892, however, every Indian at the mouth of the Berens River was officially reported as Christian.

Inland the process of conversion was very slow. From 1904 until 1916, 70 to 90 percent of the Little Grand Rapids Band were still reported as adherents of aboriginal beliefs. As for the Ojibwa farther inland at Lake Pikangikum, the Reverend Arthur Barner, writing in 1930, asserted that there was not one nominal Christian in the band when he visited them nine years before. So it is not surprising that as late as 1934, two years after I visited them, 14 percent of this band were reported as entertaining "aboriginal beliefs."

One of the consequences of Christianization, of course, was the decline of polygyny or the taking of multiple wives, an institution that once flourished among both the Cree and Ojibwa of the Lake Winnipeg region. It is probable, however, that at most, no more than 20 percent of the men were ever polygynous and that few men had more than two or three wives. One man in my genealogies had six and this was considered phenomenal. By 1876, there is evidence from treaty records that the practice was on the decline. The groups in which polygynous marriages occurred constituted only 39 percent of the native population within the area covered by the Lake Winnipeg Treaty. The increasing moral pressure exerted by the missionaries made the formal contraction of new polygynous unions impossible. The missionaries' insistence that individuals who desired to become full-fledged Christians abandon all wives but one, combined with the death of polygnous men, or their wives, of an older generation, also led to the gradual extinction of this aboriginal institution. There was no governmental interference until 1895, when the Department of Justice ruled that Indians were liable to the same penalties for polygyny as non-Indians.

POLITICAL DEVELOPMENTS

The other major influence directly affecting the Indians of the Lake Winnipeg region emanated from political events and the white population movements closely associated with them. Actually, the Dominion emerged slowly. The older provinces of Upper and Lower Canada were not united as the Province of Canada until 1841. It was not until 1846 that the Oregon Treaty established the 49th parallel as the U.S. boundary from the Rocky Mountains to the Pacific. Only a few years thereafter did Vancouver Island and later the mainland become British colonies. At the time of Confederation in 1867, approximately 80 percent of a population of over three million lived in Ontario and Quebec. Among other things, Confederation became the instrument of the western expansion of the white population of the Dominion into the prairie provinces, where between the Red River Valley and the Pacific coast there had been no white settlements before. This movement of population lagged far behind the advancing frontier in the United States, where the view that it was the "manifest destiny" of the nation to occupy the continent from coast to coast was clearly articulated by the 1840s, and where the discovery of gold in California speeded the settlement of the Pacific coast by the end of that decade.

One of the major steps that had to be taken before the Dominion of Canada could be extended westward was negotiation to legally extinguish the long unshaken charter rights of the Hudson's Bay Company to Rupert's Land. It has been estimated that an area of 2,500,000 square miles was involved, a large slice of the 3,851,809 square miles of land and fresh water that make up the Canada of today. In 1870, a payment of £300,000 was made to the company, which was allowed to retain the lands around its 120 trading posts; and permission was given to carry on the fur business without the imposition of any exceptional taxes. Nevertheless, the Gentlemen Adventurers of England Trading into Hudson's Bay (HBC) ceased to exist in its traditional chartered monopoly form, although the fur trade continued.

In 1870, after the Red River Métis under Louis Riel failed in their attempt to maintain an independent government, the people of the Red River settlement entered Confederation as the tiny province of Manitoba, the first province created under the new Dominion government. For a time Manitoba was often called the postage stamp province because at first it only covered an area of 11,000 square miles, its northern boundary traversing the lower part of Lake Winnipeg. Its population comprised approximately 12,000 persons, only 13 percent of whom were white; 5 percent were Indians, and 82 percent were of mixed blood. To the north and west lay the vast reaches of the North-West Territories, with their sparse, nomadic, Indian population and scattered white traders.

The Indians of the Lake Winnipeg basin were among those most rapidly brought into formal relations with the Dominion government, under the terms of the British North America Act, which charged it with the administration of Indian affairs. William Berens was about five years old when the new province of Manitoba came into existence. In the winter of 1870, his father was working for the Hudson's Bay Company at White Dog House on the Winnipeg River. William remembered that it was here that he first saw cattle and that Dr. John Christian Schultz, allied with the Canadian party in the Red River settlement, camped at White Dog on his way east after escaping from being jailed by Riel. Schultz was later knighted and served as lieutenant-governor of the province in 1888–1895.

When the Manitoba legislature first met in 1871, it was composed of men typical of the new frontier. Moccasins could be seen on many feet; the Cree and French languages mingled with English; and rough suits, bright shirts, and gay sashes were à la mode. By 1881, the population of the province had increased by 40,000, as a steady influx of settlers, mainly Ontario British, arrived to take up homesteads under the Dominion Lands Act of 1872. In the same year (1881) the eastern and western boundaries were extended to include all the new settlements that had sprung up, and the northern boundary was advanced to 53 degrees north latitude, which included the mouth of the Berens River. In 1912, the boundaries of Manitoba were expanded farther north to reach Hudson Bay and to encompass the 251,000 square miles of land and water seen on modern maps.

All the events precipitated by Confederation occurred within the lifetime of William Berens. The period in which he lived was one in which the cumulative consequences of the fur trade were combined with the Christianization of the Indians and the formalizing of relations with the government. Although his home was in the wilderness, as he was growing up he became aware of many external events as information reached him through his parents and his own experience. He once said to me, "I used to hear my mother talking about Victoria—a great queen—and this was the Christian name of my grandmother. I found it strange that a woman was the head of men and everything else and that she was going to buy this country" [Berens 1940]. Even as a boy, and later as a man, William saw more of the world beyond the Berens River than many Indians. He made his first trip to Winnipeg with his father when the latter drove a train of dogs there to collect the Christmas mail for the Hudson's Bay Company. This trip must have taken place between 1876 and 1880. His father took him to call on Ebenezer McColl who was the superintendent of Indian agencies in the Lake Winnipeg area.[2] The following summer he made another trip to the city, by canoe this time, and had his first drink of brandy while working in the lake port town of Selkirk.

By this time Winnipeg was a flourishing town that was soon to become the first metropolis west of the cities of the older Canadian provinces. It symbolized the westward expansion and growth of Canada as a nation. When the original province of Manitoba was created, Winnipeg was only a crude little village where the store houses of the free traders had sprung up in the early 1860s. Squeezed into the angle between the Red and Assiniboine Rivers, it was an unimportant sector of the larger Red River Colony. After 1870, however, it grew rapidly and prospered. In 1873, it was incorporated as a city and merged with the population around Fort Garry, the center of the Hudson's Bay Company's business. Between 1875 and 1881, the population increased to 8000. Until 1875, business remained chiefly centered on the fur trade. York boats still came in from Hudson Bay in June and returned in the fall, but the Hudson's Bay Company was already beginning to replace them with steamboats. As the company and other businesses diversified, a new commercial order was arising. Winnipeg soon became an emporium facing west as settlers from the east pushed westward in larger and larger numbers into the prairie country. They outfitted themselves in Winnipeg, to which speculators in land also flocked. The commercial future of the city became assured when it became certain in 1881 that the main line of the Canadian Pacific Railroad would pass through it [Bellan 1978]. When I first visited Winnipeg in 1930, it was a city of 217,000 people, fourth in size in the Dominion. At this time the population of the extended province of Manitoba was 700,000.

When William Berens was a boy, the Indians of the Lake Winnipeg region were chiefly concerned with the direct consequences of the new Dominion government's having assumed responsibility for the native population of the area. For the first time the Indians were brought into direct contact with the national government of a white nation, to whose sovereignty they were asked to submit without receiving franchise except under defined conditions. Although their sociocultural systems had long been influenced by the fur trade and Christianity, the Indians had remained politically autonomous. Now that autonomy was ending.

From the earliest period of colonization in North America, the British recognized the rights of the Indians to the land they occupied [but cp. Dickason 1989:233–239]. A Royal Proclamation of 1763 provided that no Indian could be dispossessed of his lands without his consent and the consent of the Crown. This high policy gave rise to the practice of making agreements, or treaties as they were later called, with the Indians. When the Earl of Selkirk visited the Red River Colony in 1817 and entered into negotiations with the local Cree and Ojibwa for the extinction of their title to the land, he was following this policy and the land was surrendered to King George III [Morris 1880:14–15].

Since the administration of Indian affairs was placed squarely upon the shoulders of the Dominion government by the British North America Act, an already well-established policy required that steps be taken to formalize the surrender of Indian interest in the land. Consequently, a series of agreements with the Indians of the west was initiated within a few years after Confederation. Treaty 1 was negotiated with the Cree and Ojibwa of southern Manitoba, the area where white settlements had multiplied and one of the regions into which the Ojibwa had expanded in the 18th century. A thousand Indians gathered at Lower Fort Garry on the Red River in August 1871 to negotiate this treaty. In general, the terms of these agreements bound the government to set aside reserves and provide other benefits, such as cash payments, annuities, supplies, educational facilities, and other considerations. In return, the Indians were to pledge peace and acceptance of the white man's rule, and to relinquish any legal claims to the lands they had formerly occupied [Morris 1880:25–40].

THE LAKE WINNIPEG TREATY

The Ojibwa both east and west of Lake Winnipeg and the Cree to the north were adherents to Treaty 5 (see map), negotiated in 1875 when William Berens was about 10 years old. It always remained a memorable event to him because his father was elected a "chief" and signed the treaty. The geographic boundaries ceded to the Canadian government by the Lake Winnipeg Treaty embraced an area estimated at 100,000 square miles. The density of the population was only 0.028 persons per square mile, the same as the estimate of Kroeber [1934:5] for the eastern subarctic region in general. Although reserves, calculated on the basis of 160 acres per family of five, were to be set up, the Indians were specifically granted "the right to pursue their avocations of hunting and fishing throughout the tract surrendered as herein before described, subject to such regulations as may from time to time be made" by the Dominion government [Morris 1880:346]. In effect, this meant that although permission to exploit the economic resources of the country or to establish settlements was left to the discretion of the government, for the time being the Indians were free to make their living as before.

Besides this, the Lake Winnipeg Treaty provided $500 annually to the band for the purchase of ammunition and twine. Although the use of guns must have supplanted the bow and arrow by this time, Chief Berens told me that his grandfather, Bear, used the bow and arrow for hunting moose, and his father employed this weapon to shoot partridges, and even muskrats and rabbits. But ammunition was expensive and a small supply of it to each man provided a necessary minimum for hunting large game since fur trapping did not provide all the meat habitually eaten. The provision of twine by the government, however, must have put an end once and for all to the women's spinning of cord from native plants. The traders, of course, had carried netting line and twine in their stock for over a century, but an annual supply that could be depended on must have made its manufacture by the Indians themselves completely superfluous. The use of nets was an integral part of their old ecological adaptation, especially during the months of open water when fish rather than game was a staple food. But a plentiful supply of netting twine probably made it possible to manufacture large gill nets with ease, making use of netting shuttles of a type acquired from the whites and familiar in Europe.

The government also agreed to maintain schools, "whenever the Indians of the reserve shall desire it" [Morris 1880:346]. At the mouth of the Berens River the first school was initiated as part of the Methodists' missionary program prior to Treaty 5. But a full-time day school was not begun until 1884. On the other hand, the introduction or sale of intoxicating liquor, which had been an integral part of the older fur trade era, was strictly forbidden. Annuity payments of $5.00 each to every man, woman, and child were part of the agreement; "chiefs," however, received $25.00 and subordinate officers or councillors $15.00.

Although it was known ahead of time that representatives of the government would negotiate with the Ojibwa of the Lake Winnipeg area at the mouth of the Berens River in the early fall of 1875, no precise date was set. So during the course of the summer, Indians from Jack Head across the lake, from Poplar River to the north, and from the Bloodvein River to the south, as well as Ojibwa residing inland began to gather. "Meetings occurred almost every day," William Berens told me in 1940. "I was pretty sure that something important was going to happen but I did not understand what it all meant." He recalled being suddenly awakened on the morning of September 20th—and he was quite correct in this—by a sound he had never heard before. He was a little scared because he thought it might be the cannibal

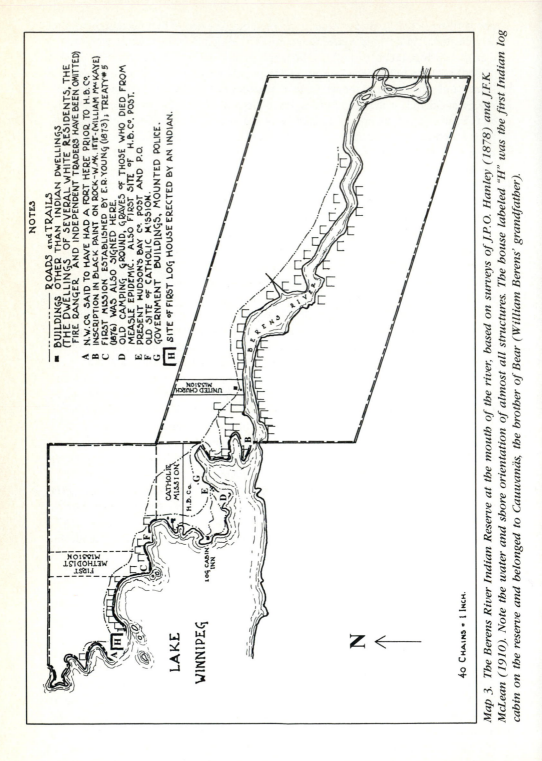

NOTES

■ BUILDINGS and TRAILS
■ BUILDINGS OTHER THAN INDIAN DWELLINGS
(THE DWELLINGS OF SEVERAL WHITE RESIDENTS, THE FIRE RANGER AND INDEPENDENT TRADERS HAVE BEEN OMITTED)

A N.W. Cº SAID TO HAVE HAD A FORT HERE PRIOR TO H.B. Cº.
B INSCRIPTION IN BLACK PAINT ON ROCK–W.M. ITIT–(WILLIAM McKAYE)
C FIRST MISSION ESTABLISHED BY E.R. YOUNG (1873); TREATY #5 (1876) WAS ALSO SIGNED HERE.
D OLD CAMPING GROUND, GRAVES OF THOSE WHO DIED FROM MEASLE EPIDEMIC. ALSO FIRST SITE OF H.B. Cº POST.
E PRESENT HUDSON'S BAY Cº POST AND P.Q.
F OLD SITE OF CATHOLIC MISSION.
G GOVERNMENT BUILDINGS, MOUNTED POLICE.
H SITE OF FIRST LOG HOUSE ERECTED BY AN INDIAN.

Map 3. The Berens River Indian Reserve at the mouth of the river; based on surveys of J.P.O. Hanley (1878) and J.F.K. McLean (1910). Note the water and shore orientation of almost all structures. The house labeled "H" was the first Indian log cabin on the reserve and belonged to Cauwanâs, the brother of Bear (William Berens' grandfather).

34

monster *(windigo)* his grandmother had told him about. It was the whistle of the S. S. Colvile, a new steamer that the Hudson's Bay Company had placed at the disposal of the treaty party. No steamboat had ever entered the river before, and it was whistling for a pilot. His father and four other Indians immediately rowed out in a skiff to meet it. The Indians met the officials at the Wesleyan Mission school house, which had been offered them by the Reverend E. R. Young, the resident missionary. The first thing the interpreter said was, "Our great mother Queen Victoria has sent us to make a bargain with you about your country." Then small hams were distributed and flour to make bannock. The meeting and feasting went on all day, and the actual treaty papers were not signed until midnight. When he awoke the next morning, William said, "I saw some new clothing lying there by my father—a red fancy coat, dark blue pants, socks, and boots. There was also a flag and a medal! I heard people say then that my father had been elected chief. Before this time the only chiefs were the fur-chiefs, the best hunters, appointed by the Hudson's Bay Company" [Berens 1940].

THE NEW ORDER: CHIEFS AND BANDS

Jacob Berens previously had held no position of power or authority within the structure of Ojibwa social organization. For among the Northern Ojibwa, at least, there were no "chiefs" in the usual political meaning of this term. The "chief" and "councillors" instituted by the Lake Winnipeg Treaty, like the "bands" that soon emerged, were devices introduced by the government as a convenient means of dealing with Indians whose native culture did not function through persons whose role it was to represent them in transactions with outsiders. The problem of designating chiefs had emerged during the negotiations for Treaty 1 (1871) at Red River, when some Indians denied that the signers of Selkirk's Treaty (1817) were chiefs or had any authority to sign the treaty that was made [Morris 1880:25, 33]. So the procedure followed in many later negotiations was to have the Indians elect representatives on the spot. The balloting at Berens River, I was told, was carried out by having each voter walk up to the table where the officials sat and place a stick in a receptacle to his right or left, each receptacle having been previously identified with one of the two candidates. It was in this way that Jacob Berens became the officially recognized representative of the Berens River Indians, and he signed Treaty 5.

The representative principle was clearly recognized by Alexander Morris, Lieutenant-Governor of Manitoba and the North-West Territories, who negotiated the treaty. In his published account he pointed out that the salary paid to chiefs and councillors made them "officers of the Crown" [1880:286], although the duties of such persons were never clearly defined. Thus, although these men became the chosen representatives of local groups of Indians in transactions with the government and enjoyed a certain prestige, such chiefs had little authority in dealing with local matters within the "bands" they represented. The bands were likewise groups created by the treaties and they arose and developed as a consequence of the new relations between the native population and the Dominion government. Consequently, both at the time of the treaties and later, these bands, considered as administrative units and supervised by government agents, must be clearly distinguished from the structures and functioning of various groups that were rooted in the aboriginal culture of the Indians, with which they did not coincide.

In everyday life, at the local level, many traditional institutions continued to operate without drastic changes, despite the new arrangements that had been imposed. In addition, the men who according to aboriginal beliefs had "power" (but not institutionalized authority for making legislative, judicial, or penal decisions affecting their fellow men) continued to exercise it. These were the so-called medicine men, who because of esoteric experiences acquired in dreams were greatly feared, as well as revered, because they could not only cure the illness of others but sorcerize them. The social influence these medicine men could exercise was grounded in the fact that they held in their hands the power of life and death. At the time of the Lake Winnipeg Treaty some of these men attempted to enhance the power reputedly derived from other than human sources by seeking election to the position of chief in order to gain the prestige that accrued to this new position.

Peter Stoney, for example, an Ojibwa from the Bloodvein River region, was a leader of the Midewiwin, a role likewise played by his father and father's brother. He wore his hair in long braids and never was converted to Christianity. One of my informants told me about a miracle he had seen Peter Stoney perform during the course of a Midewiwin held at Jack Head. Peter sharpened a stick and then walked up to one of the other *mide* priests. The latter stuck his tongue out. Peter spitted the man's tongue with the stick and cut it off with his knife. He then circled the lodge exhibiting the spitted tongue, after which he returned to the man whose tongue he had cut off and replaced it. It was Peter Stoney who was Jacob Berens' rival for the chieftainship in 1875 and later Stoney became chief of the Island bands to the south. He was considered to be so powerful that when subsequent to the election Jacob Berens became ill, it was thought that Peter Stoney had sorcerized him in retaliation for defeat. We have a clue here about why several medicine men were elected chiefs by both Cree and Ojibwa adherents to Treaty 5. Men of this category had also been appointed as "fur chiefs" by the Hudson's Bay Company during a previous period. On account of the reputed power of these "fur chiefs" some of the Indians were afraid to oppose them once it was known they desired any office because they were, in effect, the most influential personages in the older system. On the other hand, since Jacob Berens was a Christian, his election epitomized the acculturative influence that anticipated future developments.

At the time Treaty 5 was signed, a formal unity was imposed upon the Ojibwa on the eastern side of Lake Winnipeg by having Jacob Berens represent those living on the Poplar River to the north, as well as the Ojibwa who inhabited the upper reaches of the Berens River. This inland population was represented by a single councillor under Chief Berens, and the Poplar River people by another, whereas two councillors from the mouth of the Berens River were appointed. The year after the treaty was made 668 persons received annuities, a figure that indicates the sparsity of the population at that time, as well as the size of the group that Jacob Berens represented. This group, of course, did not constitute a "tribe" in any sense. Nor was it a localized group or a community composed of persons all related by blood and marriage. The Poplar River was miles to the north and the Ojibwa up the Berens River at Pikangikum were about 250 miles inland. The only ground for unification lay in administrative convenience and the fact that these people shared a common language and culture. But when reserves came to be laid out and the Indians began to build log homes on them, the reserves increasingly became the local centers of subgroups that were then given administrative recognition as "bands," each having its own chief and councillors. These bands, although not explicitly corresponding to any aboriginal group, did embrace persons within a given local area, including a number of different winter hunting groups and groups that during open water camped at established fishing places and among whom there was considerable social interaction.

The Ojibwa of the Poplar River became constituted as an independent band, as did the Little Grand Rapids Band with a reserve a little over 100 miles up the Berens River on Family Lake, and the people at Lake Pikangikum about 150 miles farther inland. Reserves for these last two bands were not laid out until the 1880s. William Berens as a young man was employed by the surveying party that laid out the Pikangikum reserve in 1888. In 1892, official census figures, enumerating the population of these bands and including information on religious affiliation, were first published. On the Berens River the band at the river mouth, Little Grand Rapids, and Pikangikum continued to encompass the Indian population of this region in the 20th century. In 1934, the population of these three bands was 891.

The Indian population within the boundaries of the Lake Winnipeg Treaty has continually increased. According to official census figures, the Indian population of the Berens River doubled in numbers between 1901 and 1934. Although the Berens River Band proper, at the mouth of the river, increased in size during the late 19th century, the increase on the river as a whole in this century is primarily attributable to the population growth of the two inland bands. My genealogies showed the average number of offspring per fruitful woman to be 4.5. In fact, 54.7 percent of the women of this category had more than three children. I mention these facts because they are not a purely local phenomenon. Other data likewise indicate that population increase, rather than decrease, has been characteristic of the period during which the Dominion government assumed responsibility for Indian affairs. Today the Indians are the fastest growing ethnic group in Canada.[3] In the province of Manitoba, the Indian population in 1934 was 12,958, whereas in 1958 it was 22,077, an increase of 70.4 percent. Dunning in his analysis of the Berens River data saw "a close correlation between the rise of population and the increase of subsidies in the form of rations, and later of direct cash subsidy." Since there was no evidence to indicate an increase in the birth rate, population increase, he pointed out, was only limited by the relation between the rate of natural fertility and the death rate [1959:52–54].

SUBORDINATION, INTEGRATION, AND CONTINUITY

From the time of Confederation forward, the Indians of the Dominion, through treaties and acts of parliament, increasingly became involved in two sociocultural systems, although at the local level participation had begun to affect their daily lives long before. In the beginning, however, the sociocultural systems of the Indians were politically independent. The first change occurred when the technological and economic aspects of their aboriginal mode of adaptation were modified by contact with the system of business enterprise represented by the fur companies with their European cultural tradition. A further step toward change occurred when the Indians were confronted by a Christian world view through the deliberate efforts of missionaries to convert them. Superficially, at least, this effort proved highly successful, although the rapidity of the process in different localities varied widely. The last step, which occurred under conditions that provided no opportunity for choice, was more drastic in its implications. Few Indians could have appreciated the ultimate totality of its consequences. For what they were asked to do, through formal agreement, was to give up forever all legal claims to the great majority of the lands they occupied, as well as to become subject in the future to the decisions of a national state and the goals and values that determined them, without being given, at first, any effective means of influencing such decisions. Today the integration of Indians into the mainstream of Canadian life is the aim of government policy while it recognizes their right to maintain their own cultural identity [Hawthorne, ed. 1966:10; 1967:28].

When considered in historical perspective, this increasing participation in two sociocultural systems, requiring as it did changing forms of social and cultural integration at the local level, and eventuating in the political subordination of the Indian to the Euro-Canadian system, permits two major points of emphasis:

1. Analysis of the conditions and events of an acculturative process that led to the increasing acceptance of more and more features of the sociocultural system of the economically and politically dominant whites as a reference group, with the concomitant disappearance of the vestiges of the most characteristic features of the aboriginal systems
2. Emphasis upon the persistence of continuities of the native sociocultural systems because influences from the past by no means suddenly disappeared

Abstractly considered, both points of emphasis are necessary for a complete understanding of the total historical process. At the same time, since the rate of change varied in different localities, variations in the patterns of integration that were manifest among different Ojibwa groups make some choice of emphasis possible, particularly in those cases where the rate of change was relatively slow. Having indicated in broad outline the historical framework that gave rise to the major categories of change among the Northern Ojibwa, I wish in Chapters 4–6 to emphasize the cultural continuities that linked the Berens River Ojibwa to the past and served to maintain their cultural identity, rather than to attempt to analyze all the specific changes in the direction of acculturation that were occurring at the time of my fieldwork in the 20th century.

EDITOR'S NOTES

1. The Norway House Methodist baptismal register (no. 1110) records the baptism of Jacob Berens by McDougall on 25 February 1861, but there is no firm evidence that Berens participated in the Ojibwa

delegation that visited Young in the summer of 1871. His Hudson's Bay Company employment, however, frequently brought him to Norway House, and he probably met the Youngs on various occasions before they moved to Berens River.

2. In the fall of 1877, Ebenezer McColl arrived in Winnipeg to investigate "certain frauds and irregularities" in the administration of J.A.N. Provencher, who had been acting superintendent of Indian affairs for Manitoba and the North-West Territories; it may have been in that winter that the Berenses called on McColl. He remained as superintendent and inspector of Indian affairs in Manitoba for the rest of his career, and William Berens formed a high opinion of his qualities (McColl 1989).

3. Recent studies show that Canada's native population declined until 1920, then began to increase at a rate higher than that of the overall population. Annual Indian population growth peaked at almost 4 percent in the late 1950s and has since declined. In 1986, Statistics Canada reported 93,000 native people in Manitoba, constituting 9 percent of the population (Gottesman 1988). Problems of enumeration and definition, however, complicate the picture, particularly for Métis and nontreaty Indians who may elect or be assigned to a variety of ethnic identities.

PART TWO

ADAPTATION, CULTURE, AND RELIGION

4 / Ecological Adaptation and Social Organization[1]

SEASONS AND SUBSISTENCE

The traditional manner of life characteristic of the Berens River Ojibwa is permeated with linguistic, social, and cultural features that reflect the ecological adaptation they have made to the climate and topography of the Canadian Shield. Although this physical environment should be considered a limiting rather than a determining factor, its basic influence has remained relatively constant despite acculturation. Native terms in the lunar calendar and for seasons of the year reflect awareness of recurrent natural changes and serve to orient activities in an annual cycle. Temperatures, for example, range from –20°F in winter to +72°F or more in the hottest part of the summer. Ojibwa terminology punctuates the consequence of these changes in temperature as it affects the Indians' terrain and livelihood: the arrival and departure of migrant birds, the seasonal habits of fur-bearing animals, and the yearly round of economic activities.

Summer, in Ojibwa terminology, covers our months of June, July, and August, corresponding precisely to the period when temperatures are the highest. And Freezing-Over Moon (November) in the lunar calendar signifies the advent of winter. Even before this time, snow, averaging perhaps 50–100 inches during the winter, may begin to cover the forests. Mid-Winter Moon (February) coincides approximately with the lowest temperatures. Although the snow may begin to melt in April, called Goose Moon because these migrant birds are first seen about this time, it does not disappear entirely until early May when the ice breaks up. May is the Moon of the Loons, and several months of open water follow. The appearance of leaves on the deciduous trees is referred to by the moon name for June, which heralds the coming of the summer season.

Correlated with these fluctuations in physical environment, we find not only changes in Ojibwa occupations but seasonal movements of the population, which have roots in the distant past and in aboriginal culture. The Ojibwa have been characterized until very recently by the fact that they occupied no fixed settlements the year round. Schoolcraft drew attention to this fact as early as 1834. On this account the size, composition, organization, and functioning of Ojibwa social groups must be conceptualized in relation to seasonal movements of population. And their sociocultural system must be primarily thought of as functioning in terms of relatively small face-to-face localized groups correlated with these seasonal

43

movements and the economic activities associated with this basic ecological adaptation. The face-to-face group that was the effective unit of social and economic organization at all seasons was the extended family.

The late fall, winter, and early spring were the seasons for hunting and trapping. During this period the characteristic localized unit of population was what I shall call the *winter hunting group*. When the ice broke up, members of such groups moved their camps to traditional places where fishing was good. Having been relatively isolated during the winter months, they now joined members of other hunting groups. These new concentrations of population during open water were larger in size and somewhat different in composition from the *winter hunting groups*. I shall call them *summer fishing settlements*. The population movements of the Ojibwa involved a maximum dispersal of small localized population units during the season of hunting and trapping and relatively larger concentrations of population during the season of open water when fishing became a major activity. Except in the most acculturated band at the mouth of the Berens River, this was still the basic pattern during the period of my observation in the 1930s.

WINTER HUNTING GROUPS

From field data collected from the two least acculturated bands of the river, Pikangikum and Little Grand Rapids, I found that the population split up into 32 winter hunting groups. The average number of individuals per group was 16, and the ratio of hunters to nonhunters was 1:3.

Typically, the winter hunting group was an extended family. It was composed of at least two married couples and their children united by kinship bonds between parents and children or between siblings. In half of such groups one or more married sons were associated with their fathers (patrilocal residence). That this was a typical pattern is shown by the fact that in cases where this association was not found, there were no married sons in the family group. In such instances, one or more sons-in-law were members of the group (matrilocal residence). Cases where *both* sons and sons-in-law were present were infrequent. Another variant of the basic pattern of the association of sons with their fathers in the winter hunting group is illustrated by cases of married brothers remaining in such a group subsequent to the death of their father. This association of closely related males in the winter hunting group is an expression of the patri-centered emphasis, which is characteristic of all the Northern Algonquians and a feature of their aboriginal culture. Since hunting is a male occupation, closely related males of an extended family were inevitably brought into close association in hunting and trapping activities. And functionally, sons-in-law could easily play the same role as sons in the winter hunting groups.

HUNTING GROUPS VERSUS HUNTING TERRITORIES

Among the Ojibwa, however, as among other Northern Algonquians, another feature characterized the functioning of winter hunting groups, although its historical roots involve a moot question. This feature was the association of each group with a delimited tract of land. For the Indians of Berens River these tracts averaged 93 square miles in area, with a range from 13 to 212 square miles. This association has been labeled a *hunting territory system* since members of the same winter hunting group return to the same territory year after year.[2] Rights to these tracts were recognized and trespass was resented. Their approximate boundaries could be easily traced by the Indians themselves. I recorded them on large-scale maps.

No rigid principles of inheritance governed the transmission of these hunting territories for such inheritance laws were not needed. Recognized rights focused upon *usufruct* (customary use), not on the possession of the land itself. The size of a tract depended upon the number of active hunters, the abundance of game, and the topography. Geographical area was of secondary importance. Any rule of primogeniture would have been impractical, and the territory of a man with half a dozen sons could scarcely have been split into economically equal parts at his death. What happened was that men who had hunted together in an established tract went on hunting there for many years. There was no pressure on them to change since other groups of hunters occupied localities elsewhere. It was inevitable, then, that a son would continue to hunt in the same territory after his father's death, just as he had hunted there prior to it and perhaps had learned to hunt there as a boy. On the other hand, a man who had hunted with his father-in-law might continue to do so after the latter's death, although not inevitably. Since a winter hunting group was never merely a single nuclear family, the association of partners followed kinship lines. The result in this patri-centered culture was that in most cases men of the same paternal lineage associated with one another for long periods, with particular hunting tracts being identified with this pattern of relationship.

What needs emphasis is the fact that, considered from a primarily economic point of view, the association of related men and their families in winter hunting groups does not necessarily involve the recognition of established rights to a specific hunting territory. Indeed, a seasonal return to the same hunting tract assumes considerable stability in the population occupying a given region. Yet the Ojibwa, as I have pointed out, are known to have undergone great geographical expansion. In the past, winter hunting groups similar in size and composition to those that I recorded moved into new regions. Evidence for these movements is found in the genealogies I collected, combined with information about the specific location of the hunting areas of a few identifiable individuals of past generations. Thus, although winter hunting groups and the hunting territory system have sometimes been considered to be interdependent variables (and for this reason the aboriginality of the latter has been asserted [Speck 1923, 1927]), this association is not inevitable.[3]

If we consider winter hunting groups and the hunting territory system as independent variables, the historical question takes another form. This question concerns the possible changing relationships between basic ecological adaptation, changing economic realities, and social organization in successive historical periods. Considered in these terms some older patterns could persist while innovations might occur. There is no reason to doubt, for example, that the characteristic kinship structure of the Northern Ojibwa, the socioeconomic role of the extended family, and the association of male kin in hunting activities persisted through both earlier and later phases of the fur trade. What has been suggested is that the hunting *territory* of the Northern Algonquians in general, as observed in operation in the 20th century, can be attributed to the influence of the fur trade.

Some evidence for this has been produced in regions other than the one under discussion here. What has been stressed are the recognized boundaries and the resentment against trespass. Of central importance, too, are the property rights of the active hunters of the winter hunting group to the exchange value, in trade goods, of the fur caught in their own traps. Certainly it is true that the proceeds from the fur catch are not shared so directly among the members of the winter hunting group as is the meat of large game animals like the caribou or moose. With the initiation of the fur trade each hunter had his own personal account with the traders and was responsible for his own "debt." Recognized rights to the tract where a man's traps were laid assumed a different economic importance because of the exchange value of the fur caught, contrasted with that of animals hunted and consumed as food. What probably happened in the Berens River region, and perhaps elsewhere, is that preceding the full crystallization of the hunting territory system, there was a period during which less exclusive rights to hunting tracts prevailed. There were hunting areas, which although they might be returned to, had less clearly defined boundaries than at a later period, or there may have been considerable movement between territories from one winter to another. I suspect that historically these variations must have been characteristic of the period of Ojibwa expansion when the Berens River Ojibwa, among others, were occupying new regions. At the same time, no tradition survives among these people of any allotment system by "chiefs" or leading men. Such men would not have had sufficient power for this.

It seems likely, then, that the institutionalization of a full-fledged hunting territory system, integrated with the seasonal dispersion of winter hunting groups, developed after the establishment of the Ojibwa population in the Berens River region. This would be a 19th-century development for the most part, during the period of closer contact with the Hudson's Bay Company and increasing dependence on trade goods. Nevertheless, the changes that occurred did not affect the basic seasonal habits of the Ojibwa in relation to their physical environment, nor did they affect the framework of their sociocultural system as a whole.

SUMMER FISHING SETTLEMENTS

In contrast to the 32 winter hunting groups of the inland bands of the Berens River, the same population during the summer was concentrated in five fishing settlements. Members of the Lake Pikangikum band were to be found in three of these, one on the lake of the same name, and the others located at Poplar Narrows on the river and at Duck Lake (Barton Lake). People of the Little Grand Rapids band resided in two summer settlements: one at Pauingassi, and the other much larger settlement near the rapids.

There was no superordinate community organization in these summer fishing settlements. Ostensibly they were simply aggregates of the members of the winter

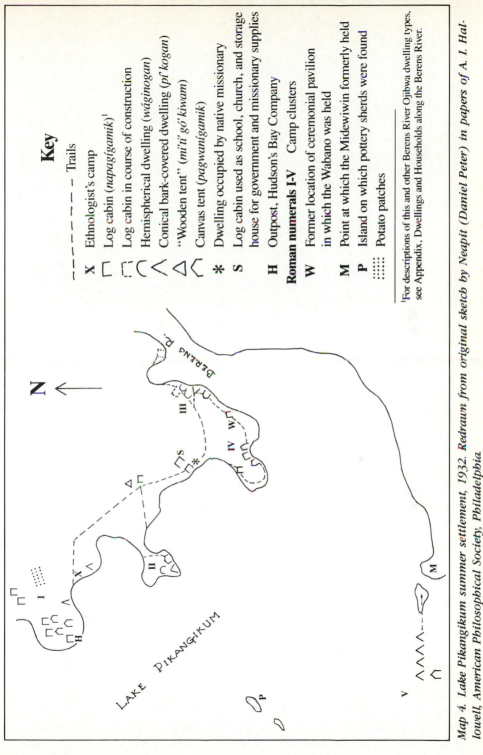

Key

– – – –	Trails
X	Ethnologist's camp
⌐⌐	Log cabin (*napagígamik*)[1]
⌐⌐	Log cabin in course of construction
⋀	Hemispherical dwelling (*wáginogan*)
⋀	Conical bark-covered dwelling (*pí'kogan*)
⊿	"Wooden tent" (*mi'ti'gó'kiwam*)
⋀	Canvas tent (*pagwanígamik*)
✳	Dwelling occupied by native missionary
S	Log cabin used as school, church, and storage house for government and missionary supplies
H	Outpost, Hudson's Bay Company
Roman numerals I-V	Camp clusters
W	Former location of ceremonial pavilion in which the Wabano was held
M	Point at which the Midewiwin formerly held
P	Island on which pottery sherds were found
⠿	Potato patches

[1] For descriptions of this and other Berens River Ojibwa dwelling types, see Appendix, Dwellings and Households along the Berens River.

N ←

BERENS R.

LAKE PIKANGIKUM

Map 4. Lake Pikangikum summer settlement, 1932. Redrawn from original sketch by Neapit (Daniel Peter) in papers of A. I. Hallowell, American Philosophical Society, Philadelphia.

Figure 7. Summer fishing settlement, probably in the Little Grand Rapids vicinity, showing a cluster of some of the dwelling types described in the Appendix.

hunting groups who camped near each other at traditional spots during the season of open water. This was the time of year when the largest numbers of Indians were to be found together, presenting opportunities for social interaction on a wider scale. Married daughters who were isolated from their parents all winter on their husbands' hunting territories might spend the summer encamped with their parents. It was at these summer encampments that the Midewiwin was formerly held, and at the time of my observations, Wabano ceremonies, dances, and occasional conjuring performances also occurred.

In the summer of 1932, for example, the largest settlement of members of the Pikangikum band, with a population of 122, was found on the lake of the same name where the reserve is located (Map 4). The Poplar Narrows settlement was a little over half as large, and the Duck Lake settlement of 50 people was the smallest. Despite the absence of any overall community organization of the summer settlements, the organization they did possess was clearly discernible at the subsettlement level. The population was not scattered at random but nucleated locally, as casual observation indicated and as mapping of the location of the dwellings and the collection of census data determined with greater precision. Little groups of dwellings of birchbark or canvas tents, but practically no log cabins, were found in clusters, spatially distinct from other clusters of dwellings, which were often a considerable distance away. One of these dwelling clusters occupied a small island offshore at a distance of perhaps two miles; the trail through the bush to another, from where I was camped, was at least a mile. The pattern of dwelling clusters for the settlement as a whole could not be seen, however, from any one point of observation. There were five of these dwelling clusters at Lake Pikangikum, at

Poplar Narrows there were two, and at Duck Lake one. Farther down the river at Little Grand Rapids there were 10 of them, although less clearly distinguishable in space. In size, these dwelling clusters of the upriver bands ranged from 10 to 50 persons, the average being 26. In the Lake Pikangikum settlement this figure was 24, and at Little Grand Rapids it was 20 persons.

The most significant social fact about this localization pattern is that these dwelling clusters were occupied during the summer months by extended families. At Pikangikum, for example, 61 percent of married sons with living fathers were associated with their male parent in the same dwelling cluster. Fifty-two percent of married daughters were associated with their fathers in a similar way. And on the island mentioned, the dwelling cluster consisted of a fraternity of three brothers and their families. Thus, in sociological terms, the dwelling clusters were equivalent to the winter hunting groups. Their residents cooperated in economic tasks and food sharing. The fact that a large proportion of the individual dwellings in each cluster were occupied by nuclear families, averaging 5.5 persons in the Pikangikum settlements and slightly fewer at Little Grand Rapids, is of subordinate importance when the functioning of the personnel of the cluster as members of extended families is taken into account.

The dwelling clusters represent actual continuity with the past. The members of a cluster at an earlier period would, in most cases, have occupied a multiple-family type of dwelling, the *cabandawan*. This older type of dwelling had more than one entrance and more than a single hearth within. An extended family lived under one roof. But the women of the nuclear families composing it were responsible for gathering their own wood and doing their own cooking. In one of the myths I collected, a series of brothers married to a series of sisters enlarges a *cabandawan* to accommodate them all. Furthermore, the multiple-family dwelling in the past was as characteristic of winter as of summer living, although I do not mean to imply that there were no other types of dwellings, such as the teepee-shaped *pi'kogan*. Even at the time of which I speak, the log cabins that some of the inland Indians had constructed on their hunting territories actually functioned as multiple-family dwellings, although this type of structure was not found among those in the summer settlements (see Appendix).

We must conclude, I think, that the personnel of the dwelling clusters in the summer, like the members of the winter hunting groups during the rest of the year, represent in microcosm the primary functioning units of the Northern Ojibwa sociocultural system. The summer fishing settlements were macroassemblages of relatively contiguous and semilocalized extended family groups that functioned as independent units in summer, just as similar groups functioned during the winter when, however, each group was completely isolated from others. Consequently, groups such as those encamped at favorable fishing places during the summer had no need for any kind of formal organization beyond that which already existed. In both seasons, too, clan ties as well as kinship provided intergroup linkages.

It was, then, the absence of any level of supragroup organization and leadership that confronted the Dominion government when it included all the Indians of the Berens River in the Treaty of 1875. I have tried to document here the forms in which this primary level of social organization persisted until recent times, despite the creation of a "band" organization as a superstructure. In this respect, however, the Berens River band at the mouth of the river presented a contrasting picture, reflecting the impact of acculturation at the level of social organization as well as in other ways. In this locality, there was a settlement occupied all the year round. No dwelling clusters were discernible, and in winter the men who hunted usually left their families behind when they visited their hunting grounds. It was here, too, that the band chief, in residence continuously, played a more influential role than those of similar status inland.

KINSHIP PATTERNS AND SOCIAL ORGANIZATION

At all seasons of the year, of course, the Indians of these semiautonomous units of population actually were part of a larger whole. Ever since they became adherents to a treaty with the Dominion government, individuals have been identified with the various bands that were set up. Before this arrangement there was nothing comparable to the modern band organization; nor was there any tribal organization to which all the Ojibwa of the region belonged. Consequently, I have emphasized the relative functional autonomy of the localized groups I observed. These may be seen as a link with the past, and even during the period of my observation the inland Indians in particular were little affected by the band organization in their everyday life. The source of the unifying factors that bound the Indians of the Berens River region together and transcended the localized groups at all seasons was the possession of a common linguistic and cultural heritage that had roots in the distant past. Among other things, this heritage included a common world view and a system of values that even at the time of my observations had not completely dissipated. Many facets of it still affected their lives.

Because the use of the native language continued, kinship terms were still used in the traditional way to address and refer to other persons in daily life. They functioned as direct guides to interpersonal relations, since customary attitudes and patterns of social behavior, including sexual and marital relationships, were implied in the use of them. Consequently, kinship terms were not merely a device for specifying the relationship of persons, but were also a means by which the normative orientation of the self in a traditional system of socially sanctioned roles and values was achieved. The Ojibwa are an example of a now generally recognized principle: kinship terms have a socially adaptive function as a signal system for discriminating among customarily distinguishable social positions, statuses, and roles in human societies. In the sociocultural system of the Ojibwa kinship terms functioned as a means of promoting orderly social interaction within the context of interpersonal relations in localized groups as well as with respect to the interaction of individuals belonging to different groups. From childhood on, kinship terms oriented individuals' behavior in a social world that embraced members of their extended family, their social interaction with persons primarily affiliated with other groups, and as we shall see, relations with other than human persons (or spiritual beings) who appeared in dreams. Kinship, as part of the common linguistic and cultural heritage of these Indians, provided the means of structuring their relations with each other wherever they were.

Besides a common kinship pattern and traditionally shared values, their cultural heritage included a clan system. Even though the clans were not as functionally important as was kinship in daily life, they did give emphasis to lineages, both real and fictitious, through the patrilineal affiliation of the individuals belonging to them. Furthermore, these clans were not localized. When moving about in summer, for example, many individuals could find members of their own clan in almost all of the settlements. Since the membership of the eight clans represented in the total population varied from over 250 individuals to fewer than a dozen, members of the largest clans, Sturgeon and Moose, were found in every settlement, whereas the Ducks were only to be met at Little Grand Rapids. Nevertheless, representatives of seven clans resided in the two summer settlements of the Little Grand Rapids band in the middle of the river, members of six clans were to be found in the three settlements of the Lake Pikangikum band, and the same number in the single settlement at the mouth of the river.

As might be expected, the traditional patterns of their social world and their seasonal movements led to intermarriage between Ojibwa of different localized groups and also between individuals belonging to the three bands on the river. My genealogical data, which includes a sample of approximately 200 marriages, suggests that in the past, intermarriage between the members of the different lineages who had migrated to the river in the late 18th and early 19th centuries tended to consolidate and expand the population of the new region to which they had moved. It also appears, however, that as time went on, there was increasing social interaction between members of the newly constituted Berens River bands and similarly organized groups outside this region. This was particularly true of the members of the band at the mouth of the river. Their location provided a better opportunity for contacts over a wide geographical area than was possible for the Indians farther inland at the same period. Under more recent conditions such contacts have become possible for individuals of all bands. However, even at the time of my own observations I recall hearing of a girl belonging to the Little Grand Rapids band who said she would never marry an Indian of her own band.

If we compare the percentages of marriages men made with women belonging to their own band (endogamous) with those made with women of other bands (exogamous), my genealogies indicate that endogamous marriages constituted by far a large majority. Nevertheless, interband marriages occurred in considerable numbers over the generations recorded. The figures for men of the Lake Pikangikum and Little Grand Rapids bands respectively are 38 and 35 percent. The proportion of such marriages by men of the Berens River band was even higher. Besides this, these men married into four times as many different bands as did the men of the inland bands. If the inlanders married women outside their own band, their mates came from other Berens River bands. The men from the mouth of the river, however, went much farther afield. Some of them married women from bands on the western side of Lake Winnipeg or south of the mouth of the Berens River. In fact, almost 10 percent of them did not marry Ojibwa women at all, but Cree women from bands north of Lake Winnipeg.

KINSHIP TERMS AND BEHAVIOR

Since the Ojibwa kinship pattern is of a well-known type, it is unnecessary to analyze it here.[4] All that is required is an understanding of three simple principles that determine the general pattern of the system and structure the basic social interaction of individuals.

First, a chief feature of this system is that there are no special terms for affinal relatives, such as mother- and father-in-law, son-in-law, daughter-in-law, brother- or sister-in-law. All persons in the social world of the Ojibwa are assimilated to classes of kin that in our kinship system fall into the category of blood relatives. Among the Ojibwa, however, any such genetic connections, although known of course, are of secondary importance. The Ojibwa use of terms has a primary social function, uncorrelated with any precise discrimination of genetic relationships except in the case of actual parents. All terms except those used to designate Ego's own father and mother are classificatory; that is, they are used for classes of kin in a widely extended sense. Thus, from the standpoint of any Ego in Ojibwa society, *all* Ojibwa are kin of some sort. They belong to precisely the same classes of kin represented as individuals in the winter hunting group, or dwelling cluster, or summer settlement, or anywhere else. Possession of a common speech and common values means that social relations are structured in a social system coterminous with the culturally constituted world of the Ojibwa as an ethnic group.

Second, a generation status is implied in the use of all terms. As a consequence, sexual relations or marriage between classes of relatives belonging to different kinship generations violate the incest taboo. This fact, combined with the existence of patrilineal clans and an awareness that it is wrong to marry anyone of the same clan, means that it is the effective operation of the kinship system rather than any rule of clan exogamy considered independently that exerts the primary normative force in Ojibwa social relations. As a matter of record, there are extremely few violations of clan exogamy in my genealogies. It is true that in several cases of father–daughter incest known to me and in the case of a man who married his stepdaughter, the taboo against clan endogamy was also violated. On the other hand, the four cases of mother–son incest I heard about did not violate this taboo. The basic consequence of the operation of Ojibwa kinship system is to limit approved sex relations and marriage to individuals of two distinguishable classes of kin in the generation of every Ego.

Third, to understand the structure of social relations through the Ojibwa kinship system requires not only an awareness of distinctions in terminology, but also a knowledge of the *contrasting* attitudes and patterns of interpersonal behavior that correlate with different classes of kin. The central feature of Ojibwa social organization lies in the integral relationship between the two classes of kin formed in Ego's generation—siblings and nonsiblings—and the reciprocal distinction made by in-

dividuals of Ego's parent's generation between the *children* of classificatory siblings of their *own* sex and the offspring of siblings of *opposite* sex. An Ojibwa child
must not only learn terminology distinctions between siblings and nonsiblings of his
own generation, associated with contrasting roles, but he must correlatively learn
that the reciprocal roles he is requested to play towards the parents of these two
classes of kin require contrasting patterns of behavior as well as terminology
distinction. Once a child becomes aware of these differential modes of conduct and
terminology and is able to act in accordance with them, his roles in the entire social
system become crystallized.

A child soon learns, for example, not only that he has many siblings but that his
father and mother likewise have many kin of the same class. He discovers through
experience, moreover, that all the men whom his father calls "brother" play a role
towards him that resembles very closely that of his own father. These "brothers" use
the same kinship terms in direct address to him that they apply to their own children.
Reciprocally, the term the child is taught to use for the "brothers" of his father has a
social connotation that is well conveyed by the English term *stepfather*. Consequently, in his own generation Ego identifies the children of these men as siblings
and uses brother and sister terms for them as they do in addressing him. In
anthropological terms, they are his parallel cousins.

It is also typical of the Ojibwa use of kinship terms that the *male* children of men
who call each other "brother" perpetuate the use of this term for each other through
successive generations. This patterning is reinforced by the patrilineal emphasis that
is characteristic of Ojibwa culture and is consonant with the typical association of
related males in the winter hunting groups as well as in the dwelling clusters of the
summer settlements. Consequently, a boy's relations with all the men his father
calls "brother," whose children are "siblings" to him, are characterized by a special
intimacy derived from experience as well as terminological usage. They form a
distinct group among the male kin of the Ojibwa boy.

At the same time, the wives of this group of men constitute a distinct class of
women in relation to any Ego. For an Ojibwa child also discovers that a corresponding kinship pattern and comparable roles likewise apply to all the women who are
"sisters" to his mother. Ego belongs to the same kinship class as the children of
these women who are "stepmothers" to him. Furthermore, these women, as the term
used for them suggests, belong to the kinship class in his parents' generation from
which Ego's mother and all the wives of the men his father calls "brother" are
drawn. Thus, terminology, status in the kinship system, attitudes, and behavior are
all integrated from the standpoint of the Ojibwa child. He discovers that in addition
to his own parents, he has stepparents; that in addition to his own brothers and
sisters he has many other siblings. All of these are his closest kin, even though in
the case of siblings all of them do not belong to his own clan. The existence of
patrilineal clans leads to one differential feature between classificatory siblings
related to Ego through the paternal line and through the maternal line. The children
of women whom a child's mother calls "sister" may be married to men of a different
clan, so that their children, because of patrilineal descent, may belong to a clan
other than his own. On the other hand, the children of one's father's "brothers"
necessarily belong to one's own clan for the same reason.

AVOIDANCE, JOKING, AND SWEETHEARTS

The mastery of a contrasting configuration of terms, attitudes, and behavior towards another category of kin is also required of the Ojibwa child. In the case of this second pattern, too, there are integral connections between a class of kin in Ego's generation and the parents of individuals belonging to this class. The child learns that the children of the women whom his father calls "sisters" and those of the men whom his mother calls "brothers" (their siblings of opposite sex, contrasted with those of the same sex as themselves) constitute a terminology class of *nonsiblings* in his own generation, or in anthropological terms, cross cousins. It is particularly important to learn how to behave properly towards these kin. Broadly speaking, the patterns of behavior that must be adopted towards them are the reverse of those expected in the social interaction of Ego with persons who are siblings to him and the parents of this class of kin.

Instead of the intimacy with which Ego can approach his "stepfathers" and "stepmothers," it is necessary, for example, to maintain social distance in relation to all the women his father calls "sister" and for whom he uses a distinct term. He must avoid women of this class as much as possible and only speak to them directly when absolutely necessary. And toward all the men his mother calls "brother," he must adopt an attitude that conveys respect; the freer kind of relationship that he has with his father or "stepfathers" is completely inappropriate toward his mother's "brothers". In the presence of kin who belong either to the class of "father's sisters" or "mother's brothers," any reference to sexual matters, particularly of a bawdy nature, must be avoided. If such conversation does occur, it is embarrassing to everyone, as once happened in my tent, full of men at the time, when a young fellow was talking freely and failed to notice that a man in the class of his "mother's brother" was there. The latter really wanted to laugh at what the young man said, but simply bent his head and looked at no one. The same pattern of verbal avoidance of sexual topics applies between men and between women of Ego's generation who are other than siblings to each other.

This broad pattern of social avoidance, of which verbal references of a sexual nature are a part, is familiar to every Ojibwa child. But it has a different context, as well. It is the pattern on which behavior between all siblings of opposite sex has been molded. Kin in this relationship never participate in common pastimes, games, or other activities together. Certain traditional games are played by boys; others are played by girls. In fact, the social solidarity that unites siblings of the same sex in many ways punctuates the patterns of avoidance that exist between those of opposite sex. Consequently, the "sisters" of Ego's father, or the "brothers" of his mother, although belonging to a different generation, exemplify in their relations with each other the same avoidance pattern with which Ego is acquainted in social relations with kin of the same class in his own generation. Thus, for a male, the avoidance of women of the "father's sister's" class simply identifies him further with the class of males in his parents' generation already referred to. And his "sisters" in the same way become identified in their conduct with their mothers and "stepmothers." In this way the avoidance patterns of successive generations are linked and integrated in the total structure of Ojibwa society. In daily life siblings of opposite sex are never seen alone in a canoe together or walking together for even the shortest distance through the bush. Similarly a man would never be seen under the same circumstance with any woman in the category of "father's sister," nor any woman with a man in the kinship class of her mother's brothers.

In contrast, what distinguishes the relations of *nonsiblings of opposite sex* in Ego's generation is that instead of a pattern of avoidance, permissiveness is not only allowed but given particular emphasis. This is accomplished by the use of a kinship term used reciprocally and solely by individuals in this kind of relationship. The term *ninam* actually signals the possibility of sexual relations and marriage. The English rendering, "sweetheart," closely approximates its Ojibwa connotation. Persons using this term between them are permitted the greatest freedom in speech and are defined as potential spouses. In the context of Ojibwa social life this freedom inevitably had a sexual focus. In the absence of any kind of organized social or economic activities in which unmarried boys and girls participated together, and in the absence of any motivation that inhibited social interaction, sex was the only common interest on which the relationship of nonsiblings could be patterned.

The verbal aspect of this permissive behavior has been labeled a "joking relationship" since the bawdiest kind of allusions are heard. Such exchanges are almost compulsive whenever "sweethearts" meet, regardless of age or marital status. Any occasion may be enlivened by the laughter of everyone present, especially when the exchanges are between men and women. Once I was trying to obtain some information on religious beliefs from a very old man whom I had never seen before. His wife and my interpreter happened to be *ninamak* (plural form) to each other. The whole session was disrupted when these elderly folk, grandparents to most of those present, began joking. When I made the trip inland in 1932 with William Berens, we had scarcely beached our canoe at Duck Lake when he established a joking relationship with a very old woman. He was 200 miles from home and his last trip up the river had been 40 years before. Yet because this woman was the sister of a man who fell into his nonsibling kin class, William Berens could established a permissive relationship with her instantaneously. It was punctated by a quick verbal exchange. "Which side of the wigwam do you sleep on?" he asked. When she told him, he said that he would be around that night. At another place we visited, a middle-aged married woman said to him, "Can you still make your way through it?" to which he replied, "The older you get the stiffer the horn." On another occasion I was included in the joking when an unmarried Indian and myself passed two young girls who were *ninamak* to him. It was they, not he, who started the fun.

Horseplay was also an aspect of the permissive pattern between "sweethearts." One informant told me that when he was a young boy his mother noticed him pushing his sister around playfully and half wrestling with her one day. She reprimanded him immediately. "Quit that," his mother said, "*she's* not (your) kinam," thus emphasizing the difference between the behavior expected between nonsiblings of opposite sex as compared with siblings. Another man told me that in the middle of a cold winter night he arrived at the wigwam where his brother and other kin were sleeping. When he entered he threw himself down beside his brother's wife and snuggled up against her under the rabbitskin blanket. Everyone woke up and there was uproarious laughter. It was part of the fun to refer to the episode later in a boastful way, saying that he had been under the blankets with his "sweetheart." Once when I wished to take a picture of an old man, I sat him on a box and started to fix my tripod. He sat with his legs wide apart. Quick as a flash, the wife of the man I was staying with—a middle-aged Christian woman and a pillar of the mission—started to laugh and made a gesture as if to unbutton the old man's fly. Everyone else laughed, too. He was her *kinam* (reciprocal term for *ninam*).

Although not encouraged, men and women in this relationship might become lovers before either of them married. But since girls as a rule married at an early age, such cases were of little importance. What requires emphasis is that after marriage it was expected that the permissive pattern of behavior between *ninamak* would be limited to bawdy talk or the kind of horseplay mentioned. The fact that all the wives of my classificatory brothers were my *ninamak* did not imply any sexual privileges. In fact, any hint of an affair with a married women of this category was considered scandalous, although not as bad as a sexual relationship with women of other kinship classes. It may also be pointed out that by and large, individuals in the *ninamak* relationship were only infrequently found in the same winter hunting group or dwelling cluster. The siblings of Ego were the most typical members of these groups belonging to the same generation. But in the summer settlements, "sweethearts" constantly met at ceremonies, dances, and on other occasions.

MARRIAGE

The parents of Ego's *ninamak,* as I have said, belonged to the kinship class of father's sisters and mother's brothers. Following marriage, of course, with any specific *ninam,* some particular man and woman in the category of Ego's parents' siblings of opposite sex became what in our conceptual scheme would be a father- and mother-in-law. Although this was a new relationship and a man was expected to help his father-in-law by hunting with him if needed, no changes in behavioral patterns were involved. The avoidance patterns already established between a man and any of his classificatory father's "sisters" continued, as did the respectful attitude towards their spouses. And since there were no special terms for affinal relatives no terminological changes were necessary. Consequently, the avoidance pattern between a woman and her daughter's husband can hardly be labeled a "mother-in-law taboo" comparable with what we find among other peoples, despite the fact that it shares some of the same characteristics. All we can say is that this pattern of avoidance among the Northern Ojibwa did not begin with marriage, and was characteristic of other relationships as well.

One way to characterize the Ojibwa kinship system is to say that it was based on bilateral cross-cousin marriage. Empirically, however, this cannot be taken to mean that most marriages involved mating between actual first cousins, that is, the children of Ego's father's sisters or mother's brothers in the genetic sense. Probably not more than 25 percent of the marriages were between individuals as closely related as this. And as I have indicated, the Ojibwa themselves did not think in these terms. Individuals were not motivated to choose first cousins as spouses. Consequently, although marriages of actual cross cousins do occur, these cannot be regarded as *preferential* marriages. It seems preferable then, to characterize the system in its own terms by saying that what it does is to identify a class of mates for Ego in every generation that includes first cousins as well as individuals more remotely related. So long as the extended incest taboos built into the system were maintained, the only possible spouses were individuals chosen within the class of potential mates thus defined.

Similar questions arise with respect to the occurrence of other types of preferential marriages—the levirate, sororate, and sororal polygyny. If the levirate is defined as the preferential marriage of a widow with her deceased husband's genetic brother, this kind of marriage occurred so infrequently among the Ojibwa that it cannot be said to be traditional or customary. On the other hand, the Ojibwa kinship system did promote the marriage of a widow with a man who belonged in the terminological class of "brother" to her deceased husband. The sororate (a man marrying his deceased wife's sister) offers a parallel case. I have no information indicating that it was a preferred type of marriage. However, I was once present when a man was discussing the possibility of a marriage between his son-in-law (a widower) and another of his daughters (the older sister of whom had been this man's first wife). I do not know whether this marriage took place.

With respect to sororal polygyny at an earlier period when plural marriages were permitted, there is some data in my genealogies, but it is ambiguous. In six out of eight polygynous marriages the husbands did have genetic sisters as wives. On the face of it this suggests preferential marriage. On the other hand, Cenawagwaskang, who belonged to one of the most remote generations recorded and was one of the oldest members of the Moose Clan inland, presents an interesting case. Although notorious because he had six wives, the largest number recalled for any man, none of them were genetic sisters, although three belonged to the same clan. A contemporary who belonged to the Sturgeon Clan and was well remembered as a prominent leader of the Midewiwin had two wives. These women belonged to different clans. If sororal polygyny was a preferential type of mating at one time, it might have been expected that these representative men of the old regime would have followed an established custom. But in these cases as well as in the other six, the wives were terminological sisters, even though they belonged to different clans.

GRANDPARENTS AND "OUR GRANDFATHERS"

The terms "grandfather" and "grandmother" and the reciprocal term "grandchild" as used by the Ojibwa signal behavioral correlates and connotations that in certain respects set these relationships apart from those already described. In daily life the social relations of children and grandparents are essentially permissive, resembling those of Ego to parents and stepparents in some respects. But there are some differences. In its degree of permissiveness, for instance, a point is reached where an old man may joke a little with his "granddaughter" even to the extent of making sexual allusions. No stepfather would go that far. At the same time, considered as a

Figure 8. Chief William Berens and "our grandfather's rock" with offerings, on portage between Poplar Narrows and Pikangikum, Berens River, probably photographed when Berens and Hallowell traveled up the river in 1932. This large, smoothly rounded boulder, similar to ones often placed in the Wabano pavilions, was revealed in a dream to a man who had placed it there a number of years before. "It is regarded as sacred and has become a shrine where passers-by often leave sacrifices of tobacco and other objects" (Hallowell n.d.:5).

mode of address, grandparent terms are used in an extended sense to include all persons in the kinship generation older than parent. These terms always carry overtones of respect, associated with advanced age, experience, and presumed wisdom. Associated with the grandparent status, too, is a special role. Personal names were once bestowed upon all Ojibwa infants by persons of the grandparent class in a traditional ceremony, which began to decline, however, with the spread of Christianity. These native names were sacred names and carried with them benefits for the child. These were derived from the contacts the namer, particularly a grandfather, had had in dream experiences with spiritual beings or other than human persons. A further link between persons of this category and human beings of the grandparent class is the fact that collectively, other than human persons were referred to as "our grandfathers." Besides this, the Ojibwa believed that they came into direct personal contact with other than human persons in their dreams. The dreamer and these persons used the kinship terms *grandfather* and *grandchild* in direct address, and the dreamer benefited from experiences of this kind.

Consequently, the relationship between grandparents and grandchildren leads directly from a consideration of the interrelated roles of the Ojibwa social structure to their traditional world view. And as we shall see, an understanding of their cognitive outlook is necessary for a comprehension of the functioning of their sociocultural system considered as a whole. The basic social sanctions involved in the maintenance of Ojibwa social structure depend upon, among other things, the culturally constituted beliefs, values, personal experience, and personality organization of individuals.

EDITOR'S NOTES

1. This chapter appeared in slightly different form as Chapter 8 in *Contributions to Anthropology: Selected Papers of A. Irving Hallowell*, under the title, "Northern Ojibwa Ecological Adaptation and Social Organization," copyright 1976 by the University of Chicago. The kind permission of the University of Chicago Press to reprint this text is gratefully acknowledged. The original typescript bore no chapter designation and was not filed with the other draft chapters of this book. It therefore seemed, at first, that the book's Chapter 4 was missing. Filed with this typescript, however, was a manuscript version marked "IV," and there is no doubt of its continuity with the rest of the chapters published here.

2. As Rogers and Taylor (1981:236) have noted, such lands "were in reality trapping territories," serving to allocate beaver and other animals trapped for fur (as well as food). They were also actually focused more along waterways than on land as such, given the aquatic orientations of beaver, muskrat, mink, and other furbearers. (This fact, obscured by our customary terminology, explains why hydroelectric developments and water pollution can be so destructive of northern native economies; see, for example, Salisbury 1986 on the James Bay Cree and hydroelectric developments in Quebec.)

3. For summaries and analyses of the complex issues surrounding the origins (and definitions) of hunting territories, see Rogers 1981: 25–26 and the essays by several authors in Bishop and Morantz, eds. 1986. Hallowell's views as expressed here may be compared with those in his earlier article (1949) on the subject, which, although it focused more on ecology than origins, followed more closely the conclusions of his mentor, Frank Speck.

4. Anthropologists describe the Ojibwa kinship pattern as bifurcate collateral, with "Iroquois"-type cousin terminology (Rogers and Taylor 1981:236). That is, distinct kinship terms are used for paternal and maternal uncles and aunts, in contrast to English-language usage, which lumps together these collateral relatives from both sides; and cross cousins (father's sister's children and mother's brother's children) are distinguished from parallel cousins (father's brother's children and mother's sister's children). This, too, contrasts with English-language usage, which being of "Eskimo" type, lacks that distinction. The Ojibwa system also emphasizes generational distinctions (Hallowell 1976b:319).

5 / World View and Behavioral Environment

The ecological adaptation, demography, and social organization already outlined represent in only the most limited fashion the substantive features of traditional Ojibwa culture. Another dimension must be added to the picture if we wish to understand Ojibwa life in a more inclusive perspective and penetrate it in greater psychological depth. For these Indians, like human beings everywhere, live in a meaningful universe enriched by imagination and symbolic thought, not in a world of bare physical objects and events, rocks and water, trees and animals, demographic relationships and kinship ties. The actualities of Ojibwa life can only be fully comprehended by taking into account the ways in which their thinking, experience, and behavior are affected by the conceptualization and interpretation of phenomena that are implicit in their traditional outlook upon the world.[1]

Human cultural adaptation always involves adjustment to a world in which man's interpretation of it is fed back into his adaptation to it. Consequently, Ojibwa beliefs, values, and goals need to be considered in relation to individual conduct and the functioning of their sociocultural system as an intelligible and rewarding way of life. We must look at the world view of the Ojibwa in order to discover the source of their characteristic cognitive orientation towards the world. However limited their reliable knowledge of the universe may be, their culture provides them with presuppositions about it on which they are compelled to think and act. An examination of this outlook provides necessary clues to the Ojibwa's basic concepts and classificatory distinctions of phenomena, what kind of events they consider vital, and an explanation of their conduct under given circumstances. Although this traditional world view was not completely intact at the time of my investigations, many aspects of their thinking and behavior still reflected its continuing influence.

One of the firmest links with the past was the persistence of Ojibwa speech. As I have pointed out, the use of traditional kinship terms continued to pattern the social relations and behavior of individuals. In a parallel way, the persistence of the native language served to maintain, however unconsciously, the concepts, connotations, and classifications embedded in speech that were consonant with the Ojibwa world view. This does not mean that the semantic content expressed in speech was unchanging, or even the prime determinant of Ojibwa thinking. Nevertheless the symbolic structure for communicating the meanings inherent in a traditional world view remained.

60

ANIMATE AND INANIMATE

One of the basic features of the Ojibwa language, which is directly related to an understanding of the premises of their world view, is the fact that although a gender distinction is not formally expressed, a grammatical distinction between "inanimate" and "animate" objects is essential. Although these labels are imposed from the outside, and the Ojibwa grammatical distinction is not fully coordinate with the natural properties of objects in a scientific classification, nevertheless we can assert that the world in which the Ojibwa live is not one in which every object, of whatever kind, is conceived of as animate. Practically all manufactured objects— tools, utensils, clothing, canoes, dwellings, and so forth—fall into the inanimate class, although pipes are treated grammatically as animate. Most plants, all fish, mammals, and human beings are both grammatically and conceptually living things, much in our own meaning of the term. Most startling is the fact that the sun and the winds also belong in this category, rather than in the class of natural inanimate objects to which we assign them. The inclusiveness of the animate category of beings sharply distinguishes the Ojibwa world view from our own. It is also significant that more than formal classification of substantives is involved; there are correlative differences in attitudes and behavior based upon traditional concepts.

What is of paramount interest is that in the Ojibwa world, conceptual entities that are not palpable natural objects at all are reified as sentient, living beings of the animate category. In addition to the fauna of their physical environment, for example, certain animals of exceptionally large size are believed to exist, despite the fact that they are seldom seen. There are Great Frogs and Big Turtles, in addition to the more readily observable smaller ones. Great Frogs are feared; no one wishes to meet one. Once when four Indians were crossing Lake Winnipeg in a canoe and landed on an island where they expected to spend the night, one of these men discovered what he interpreted as tracks of a Great Frog. His companions examined them and agreed. All of these Indians became so fearful that, although night was approaching and they had a considerable distance to paddle, they decided to leave the island at once. Although snakes are among the rarest of fauna in the Ojibwa country and small in size, there is a firm belief in the existence of Big Snakes. Several of my informants reported seeing them. One of these men was a hunter of the highest repute. The creature he saw was moving into the water. He saw the head, shaped something like that of a deer, but without horns. The snake was white around the chin and the diameter of its body was "as big around as that," he said, pointing to the stove pipe in his cabin. The Great Snake moved in a straight path, not this way and that, as the smaller snakes do.

The Thunder Birds belong to a somewhat different class of animate being. They are familiar to everyone because thunder is the sound of their flapping wings and lightning is the consequence of their blinking eyes. The slowly rolling thunder with only a few claps indicates the presence of old Thunder Birds, whereas the sharper claps are made by the wings of the younger ones. I discovered one man who claimed to have seen a young one when he was a boy of 12. It was lying on the rocks after a thunderstorm, and had long red tail feathers. Conceptually, Thunder

Birds are hawklike in form with a curved beak and feet like an eagle. Like the hawks, they kill snakes, but their particular prey are the Great Snakes. The Ojibwa despise snakes and believe that the Thunder Birds have helped rid the earth of the monster relatives of these loathsome creatures. That is why so few of the Big Snakes are now seen. It is an old custom to give Thunder Birds a ceremonial smoke when they cry, turning the pipe in all directions. Sometimes a few words are said such as, "Wait, wait, you'll frighten the children," or "go easily." To the Ojibwa mind these avian characteristics are not fanciful. They are based on the observation that Thunder Birds are only heard from late spring until early fall. So they are classified with the birds that migrate to the north and leave before winter sets in. I once compared the meterological records regarding the occurrence of thunder with the periods of bird migration and found a very high correlation.

All species of wild animals and plants are believed to be under the control of "bosses" or "owners." There is an "owner" of the bears and of beavers as well as birch trees, although these animate beings are not distinguishable by proper names of their own. It was believed that it was only by the permission of the "owners" of an animal species that individual animals could be shot, snared, or trapped by the hunters. Thus, although the Ojibwa possessed an enviable knowledge of the habits of the fauna of their physical environment and the skills necessary to make effective use of the technological equipment at their disposal, knowledge and skill were not all that was necessary to make a good hunter. Above all, it was essential to take cognizance of the "owners" of animal species and treat all the animals sought for their flesh or skins in a proper manner.

Although it was necessary, of course, to kill animals, acts of wanton cruelty were strictly forbidden. In the case of some animals, what was chiefly stressed was the treatment of their material remains in customary ways. The bones of the muskrat and beaver, for example, had to be returned to the water. The ceremonial treatment of a bear's carcass, in former times, epitomizes in more elaborate form the basic attitude held toward all the animals on which the Ojibwa depended for a living. An offering of tobacco was made and a feast held, not in honor of the animal itself, but for the "owner" of the bears. The nose might be cut off and hung on a peeled spruce pole, decorated with ribbons, and the skull was hung in a tree. Dogs were never allowed to gnaw the bones of a bear, and only men were permitted to eat the tongue and heart.

What motivated such conduct was the belief that if proper treatment was not accorded to a member of an animal species used in any way by human beings, the "owner" would retaliate by making it impossible for the hunter to catch animals of this species in the future. A simple principle of reciprocity was involved here; use of an animal by any human being involved an obligation to the controller of the species. Consequently, there was always an implicit social relationship between the hunter and the "owners" of animal species, conceived as animate beings of a certain class. This relationship was far more vital to a man, in terms of world view, than the knowledge and skills he possessed as a hunter. To be a successful hunter it was necessary to fulfil one's obligations to the "owners" of animal species. Similarly, when plants were gathered for medicinal use, a little hole might be dug in the ground and an offering of tobacco left there. The "owner" might also be addressed at the same time.

Since the phrase *world view* refers to the perspective in which people look at themselves and their surrounding world in cultural terms, we cannot impose distinctions and classifications of phenomena derived from another world view upon them if we seek to comprehend their outlook. To the Ojibwa the "owners," the giant animals, and the Thunder Birds are as much a part of their world as the animals they trap and the fish they catch. To the Ojibwa hunter, his knowledge of the habits of animals and of the best way to hunt or trap them, and his relations with their "owners" form an integral pattern that functions as an essential part of his cognitive orientation to the world in which he has to act. His beliefs and personal experiences are not compartmentalized. His behavior as a hunter is a function of reliable knowledge, beliefs, values, and experience.

Although useful up to a point, any discussion of Ojibwa culture and behavior that excludes reference to their physical environment and its fauna and flora arbitrarily limits analysis, cutting us off a priori from pursuing the behavioral implications of their world view. Insofar as we take the physical environment into account, it is more satisfactory to speak of their behavioral environment. In this more inclusive perspective the properties of objects in the physical environment of the Ojibwa become subordinate to the world perceived as a consequence of the socialization of individuals who are groomed as participants in a sociocultural system. The culturally patterned, structured, and unified aspects of the Ojibwa world view take on the psychological reality that has meaning for them and motivates much of their behavior. In this perspective, we too can better understand that reality.

It should already be apparent that the Ojibwa conception of nature and natural objects does not fit the meaning of these terms as developed in the scientific tradition of Western culture. The Sun and the Winds are animate beings of a special class, which we will presently discuss. Although a distinction between inanimate and animate classes of objects is recognized, the line drawn between them is ambiguous and is not based on naturalistic concepts. On the other hand, reified or "mythical" animals like the Great Snakes are equated with their natural counterparts from our point of view, whereas physical events such as thunder and lightning are conceptualized as due to the behavior of hawklike birds. Consequently, any attempt to order Ojibwa data in a conceptual scheme familiar to us distorts their world view and makes it impossible to understand their actual behavioral environment. Linguists long ago learned to avoid ordering their data to paradigms based on Indo-European languages, and the study of non-European cultural conceptualizations requires similar caution. For the Ojibwa a natural world of objects, sharply opposed to a world of spiritual, divine, or supernatural beings is absent. Their metaphysics of being has a different ground. The absence of a natural–supernatural dichotomy becomes clearer when we consider the nature of "persons," the most important category of beings of the animate class.

OTHER THAN HUMAN PERSONS

In the Ojibwa world view "persons" include beings of an additional class to the one they use for themselves (*anishinabek,* connoting Indians or "human beings"). The category includes animate beings to whom the Ojibwa attribute essentially the same characteristics as themselves and whom I shall call "other than human" persons. This term is more descriptively appropriate than labeling this class of persons "spiritual" or "supernatural" beings, if we assume the viewpoint of the Ojibwa themselves. It is true that these entities have more power at their disposal than human beings, and this is why the humans need the help of other than human persons in achieving their goals. Nevertheless, other than human persons cannot be set off as categorically distinct. Human beings and other than human persons constitute two classes of persons. If we label the latter supernatural beings, there is the erroneous implication that the Ojibwa themselves distinguish clearly between the natural and the supernatural. On the other hand, these beings play roles similar to entities labeled "supernatural" in other cultures. If the study of religion is thought to concern itself with man's social relations with beings beyond the limits of human society, rather than primarily with theological questions and systems of beliefs, the other than human persons of the Ojibwa world are religious figures.

What requires emphasis is that all animate beings of the human category of the Ojibwa world are unified by the possession of common attributes, although they are of many different kinds. There is a vital part of these beings that is enduring, and an outward form or appearance that may be transformed under certain circumstances. Besides this, all beings of the person category have such general attributes as intelligence, will, and a capacity for speech; consequently human persons can communicate with other than human persons. Animals such as otters, kingfishers, or whitefish are animate beings, but they do not have the essential characteristics of persons. Among other things they do not have the attribute of speech. This is one of the reasons why the "owners" of plant and animal species fall into the person class, whereas the concrete animals and plants they control do not. Other typical examples of the other than human class of persons are Sun, the Winds, and the Thunder Birds.

Some beings in this class are entirely dissociated from what we distinguish as natural objects or natural forces. *Memengwéciwak,* for instance, live on the earth and are familiar to everyone, although they are met only under unusual circumstances. They have a human form, but live within rocky escarpments on the lakes. The pictographs on the rocks are attributed to them. They are fond of fish and travel in canoes. Sometimes they are said to steal fish from the nets of the Indians. Their singing and drumming can sometimes be heard, as several informants testified. When they meet human beings they hang their heads because they have no soft part to their noses, only a hole.

Cannibal giants, *windigowak* (plural), also inhabit the Ojibwa country. They are terrifying creatures. Anecdotes are told about encounters with them, and they appear in mythology. They grow taller than the tallest trees when they shout. They have been both heard and seen. William Berens gave me an account of hearing a windigo while traveling:

> One spring there were four of us who went [musk]rat hunting together. We had two canoes. We were on our way back from Rice Lake. After we had made four portages we had to cross a lake about two miles long. After this there were two more portages, short ones. When I was running back over the last portage for my last load, I heard a shout from the direction from which we had come. I heard this shout three times. It was

something like a human voice, but much, much louder. My nephew Joe heard it too, and asked me who was calling. I told him it must be a windigo. We launched our canoes and paddled for all we were worth to strike the north branch of the river.

The next day Jacob Nanakawop and Jim Bear and his mother came through. They saw the windigo. The old lady said he was not very big. But I don't think it could have been a man. His legs were bare and he had on a rabbit skin coat [an old-fashioned article of clothing seldom worn today—A.I.H.].

It is a heroic feat of the first order to kill one. Sometimes human beings turn into cannibals. They are equally feared and often killed. In 1876, three Berens River Indians killed their mother because she manifested cannibalistic proclivities; they built a pyre and burnt her body.

A year after Treaty, when Jacob Berens was chief, a woman who thought she was turning into a windigo was killed by her three sons. The men were arrested and there was a magistrate's hearing [held by HBC factor Roderick Ross, who was also serving as Indian agent]. Jacob Berens pleaded their case saying that this was this people's belief, that they thought many more people would lose their lives if the woman was not killed, and besides, the Indians had just come into Treaty and had no chance to learn anything different. The charge of murder was not pushed against the men and the case was laid on the table. According to William Berens, it was usual to burn a windigo's body; wood was piled up over it in large quantities and a fire kept going sometimes for 24 hours—so that bones and everything were burnt to a crisp—not even a bit of blood remaining [A.I.H. research notes].

Collectively, persons of the other than human class are spoken of as "our grandfathers" because the major figures are all of the male sex. The use of a kinship term for them indicates their inclusion, as persons, in the same social world as human beings. From early childhood, the experience of Ojibwa individuals is channeled both directly and indirectly towards a knowledge of and, under special circumstances, interaction with other than human persons. These entities assume the reality of persons in their lives not only through conceptualization, but through dramatization in myths, through perception of their voices heard in the "shaking tent," and visually, in the more intimate, vivid imagery of dreams.

MYTH AND METAMORPHOSIS

Ojibwa myths are considered to be true stories, not fiction. The chief characters are immortal, other than human persons whose past adventures furnish the content of these narratives. The recitation of myths was taboo except on long winter evenings when the hunting groups were isolated in the forest, for "our grandfathers" were never talked about casually or lightly. In their most classical form the myths were acted out. The narrator, who was usually of the human grandparent class, punctuated the narratives with dramatic gestures. The voices of some of the characters like *Mikinak,* the Great Turtle, were individualized. Songs were interpolated. Thus, the narration of these stories was ritualized and, at the same time, it was a kind of invocation. For "our grandfathers" were thought to come and listen with pleasure to what was being said about them. In ancient times, one of these immortal beings is reported to have said to the others: "We'll try to make everything suit the Indians so long as any of them exist, so that they will never forget us and always talk about us."

Children, from their earliest years, become thoroughly familiar with the personal characteristics of all the other than human persons who appear in the myths. They know that the four Winds, for example, are brothers, the children of the same mother, and that the Winds separated and went to live at the four quarters of the earth. They know that North Wind is cruel to human beings, because that is what he said he would be in the myth, whereas South Wind said he would be kind. They have heard of the never-to-be-forgotten occasion when *Tcakábec,* a small but extremely powerful anthropomorphic being, set a snare in the trail that Sun regularly traveled and caught him. Darkness continued and the Indians could no longer hunt. Finally, a mouse was sent to gnaw the snare and release Sun so that he could continue his regular journeys and provide light during the day. Children learn about the Thunder Birds, too, from listening to the myths. They know that these beings do not live on this earth but in another world above it. In one myth, a young man with nine older brothers falls in love with a Thunder Bird girl, who has appeared on earth in human form. In a fit of jealousy his oldest brother "kills" her, but does not destroy her vital enduring essence. She manages to fly away to Thunder Bird Land, where her lover, with great difficulty, follows her. Here he is accepted as her husband, and does not find life very different from that on the earth. He goes hunting with his wife's father and her brothers. Their prey are the Great Snakes and Frogs, but they call them "beavers." After a time he and his wife leave Thunder Bird Land, taking her nine sisters with them. "You can take them as wives for your brothers," his wife's father says. "I'll be related to the people on earth now and I'll be merciful towards them. I'll not hurt any of them if I can possibly help it." The night before they leave there is a big dance. After reaching the earth, the whole party make their way to the place where the young man's brothers are camped. They are enthusiastically received, and the nine brothers marry the nine sisters of their younger brother's wife.

This myth reflects several vital features of the Ojibwa world view and particularly the generic attributes of persons. In many ways the Thunder Birds act as human persons do. They talk and dance and hunt. Since the Big Snakes are their prey, it is intelligible why the Ojibwa consider the Big Snakes in the same class as the smaller snakes and other animals rather than in the person category. But the status of Thunder Birds as persons is more precise than this. Their social organization and their kinship terminology are identical with those of the Ojibwa, although they live in a spatially separated world. The marriage of a series of female siblings (classificatory or otherwise) to a series of male siblings directly reflects the Ojibwa kinship pattern. In one case I recorded, six genetic brothers were married to a sorority of six sisters. Finally, Thunder Birds, having the capacity to assume anthropomorphic characteristics, are conceptualized as persons because it is possible for them to marry human beings and live on this earth.

This Thunder Bird myth, moreover, brings into focus the Ojibwa assumption that both classes of persons—human and other than human—are capable of metamorphosis. This is one of the distinctive generic attributes of persons in Ojibwa thought. So far as outward appearance is concerned, no hard and fast line can be drawn between an animal form and a human form because of this possibility. Thus, both living and dead human beings, under certain circumstances, may assume the form of animals, but animals may not assume human form. Only persons are capable of metamorphosis. One informant told me of a visit his deceased grandchild had paid him. One day he was traveling in a canoe across a lake. He had put up an improvised mast and used a blanket for a sail. A little bird alighted on the mast. This was a most unusual thing for a bird to do. He was convinced that it was not a bird but his dead grandchild who visited him in animal form.

There is an old and widespread belief among the Ojibwa that sorcerers can transform themselves into bears in order to pursue their nefarious work. There is considerable anecdotal material in the literature about "bear walkers." An old man told me how he had once fallen sick, but no medicine did him any good. For this reason and others, he believed he had been bewitched by a certain man. Then he noticed that a bear kept coming to his camp almost every night after dark. Since wild animals do not ordinarily come anywhere near a human habitation, his suspicions were aroused. So when the bear appeared one night he got up, ran outdoors, and shouted to the animal that he knew why he came. He also threatened retaliation in kind if the bear ever returned. The animal ran off and never came back. Nowadays, such anecdotes are rationalized by saying that a bear walker may be a man dressed up in a bearskin. This notion reflects a modern scepticism about the traditional belief in actual metamorphosis. The attitude of my informant, however, was classical.

Metamorphosis occurs with considerable frequency in the myths. *Wisekedjak,* whose primary characteristics are anthropomorphic, becomes transformed and flies with the geese in one story, assumes the form of a snake in another, and once turns himself into a stump. Men marry "animal" wives who are not "really" animals in Ojibwa thought. *Mikinak,* the Great Turtle, in contrast, marries a human being. It is only by breaking a taboo that his wife discovers that she is married to a being who is able to assume the form of a handsome young man. The apparent ambiguities that may puzzle the outsider when reading these myths are resolved when it is understood that, to the Ojibwa, persons are capable of metamorphosis by their very nature. The names by which some of these entities are commonly known, even if they seem to identify the characters as "animals," do not imply unchangeableness in form nor impugn their status as other than human persons.

Because they share common attributes as persons, interactions between human and other than human persons are on a different plane than the interactions that characterize the relations between human beings and the animals and plants of their physical environment (if we reduce these to simple materialistic terms). Relations between human beings and their other than human "grandfathers" are not only based on the assumption that verbal communication and understanding are possible; it is also assumed that they share a common set of values. All entities of the person category belong to the same moral world. This is why moral obligations can arise between the Ojibwa and "our grandfathers," as in the case of hunters and the "owners" of animal species. Furthermore, human beings need the help of other than human persons not only in making a living but in other ways. This is why "our grandfathers" are omnipresent in the lives of the Ojibwa and why an inclusive conceptualization of persons occupies such a central position in their world view and structures their behavioral environment in a characteristic way. To appreciate the significance of this fact we must think of these Indians not only as members of a human society but as participants, with other than human persons, in a larger cosmic society. For this broader realm of social interaction is far from being metaphorical for them.

THE SHAKING TENT

The shaking tent is one of the most familiar situations in which this level of social interaction is perceptually realized. This institution channels direct contact with other than human persons of all kinds. Its purpose is to secure help from these entities by invoking their presence and communicating human desires to them. This type of conjuring is often undertaken to secure information about the health or welfare of distant persons. I took advantage of this aspect of the ceremony on one occasion to inquire about the health of my father who was ill at the time. Another conjuring performance that I witnessed was precipitated by the fact that a young man lost consciousness twice within a few days. There was no obvious reason for this so his relatives were greatly disturbed and wanted to discover the cause of his illness. Conjuring may also be undertaken to discover lost objects or obscure causes of illness. The "souls" of living persons as well as other than human persons may be brought into a conjuring lodge; and so may the "souls" of the dead. Since it is always the vital part of a person that is invoked, the living presence of persons of either class is always made manifest detached from outward form.

When a conjuring performance is to be undertaken in summer, a barrellike framework of poles about seven feet high is set up outdoors and covered with birchbark, skins, or canvas (Figs. 9, 10). In winter, of course, it must be set up inside a dwelling. After dark the conjurer enters this structure; the audience gathers outside. The conjurer invokes his particular benefactors among other than human persons, that is, his *pawaganak* or "guardian spirits." Upon their arrival the structure becomes agitated and sways from side to side. In fact, it is seldom still. It is from this fact that the English term, "shaking tent," has been used as a label for such performances. The Ojibwa say that the Winds are responsible for this agitation; the lodge is never shaken by human hands. In the past, the movements of this structure assumed a mysterious aspect because conjurers were sometimes bound with rope before entering it. Yellow Legs, the great-grandfather of William Berens, is said to have had four structures built on one occasion. He put an article of his clothing in three of them and entered the fourth. As soon as he was inside, all four lodges began to shake.

The other than human persons invoked manifested themselves vocally in differentiated voices. Sometimes they named themselves, or sang a song. From an informant of about 70 years of age, I obtained a list of all the other than human persons he recalled having heard in the shaking tent. These included the "owners" of 22 species of mammals and fish, five prominent characters in the myths, and

Figure 9. Constructing a shaking tent at Little Grand Rapids. Other photos of the same structure appear in Hallowell 1942:plate 1.

Figure 10. The shaking tent upon completion.

several semihuman entities such as *Memengweci* and *Windigo*. Members of the audience could easily recognize characters from the myths because the intonation of the voices heard issuing from the shaking tent had the same characteristics as those used by the narrators of the myths. Direct communication between members of the audience and the other than human persons present sometimes took place. At one of the performances I attended, several members of the audience called for *Mikinak*, a character in mythology. He is easily identifiable because he speaks in a throaty, nasal voice—somewhat like Donald Duck of movie fame. Anyone could address *Mikinak*, and he always had a witty answer ready. He struck a note of levity, appreciated by the Ojibwa on occasions that were otherwise serious in purpose. But no matter what the ostensible purpose of any particular performance, the presence of other than human persons in the shaking tent, where they could be heard by every man, woman, and child, served to reinforce their reality as living beings in the Ojibwa social world.

Social interactions between human and other than human persons might also take place in everyday life. These interactions demonstrate even better the psychological depth and behavioral consequences of the Ojibwa world view because of their occurrence outside any institutionalized setting like the shaking tent. A legendary anecdote, for example, recounts how two old men, noted for their own power, once vied with each other in influencing the movements of Sun:

> The first old man said to his companion: "it is about sunrise now and there is a clear sky; you tell Sun to rise at once." So the other old man said to Sun: "My grandfather, come up quickly." As soon as he had said this, Sun came up into the sky like a shot. "Now you try something," he said to his companion. "See if you can send it down." So the other man said to Sun: "My grandfather, put your face down again." When he said this, Sun went down again. "I have more power than you," he said to his companion. "Sun never goes down once it comes up."

Another anecdote about an old man named Fair Wind, with whom I was acquainted, was related to me by an eyewitness. Fair Wind was sitting in his tent one day when a severe thunderstorm came up. After an extremely loud clap of thunder and flashes of lightning, Fair Wind turned to his wife and said, "Did you understand what he said to me?" (alluding of course to the Thunder Bird, but deliberately avoiding mention of the name of this being). "Not very plainly," the old woman replied. "He's asking me whether I have a pipe and why I don't light it," Fair Wind said. "See whether you can find it for me, and hurry up about it." (This was because Fair Wind was blind.) So the old woman hunted around and found his pipe and tobacco bag. When his pipe was lighted, the old man took a few puffs and then bowed his head saying, "Here it goes." Then he slowly turned the pipe clockwise in all directions in ceremonial fashion. Everyone present was extremely solemn, my informant reported. Although he did not recall the additional words spoken by Fair Wind, he said the latter asked to be pardoned and for merciful treatment.

I was present myself one summer when a less dramatic episode occurred that indicated how directly and personally the Indians may interpret their relations with the Thunder Birds. A Wabano ceremony had started at the Pauingassi settlement, but the weather was extremely threatening. Since this affair was carried on in an uncovered pavilion of poles (Fig. 11) and would continue for three days, good weather was essential. After the drumming started, the wife of the leader, who was one of Fair Wind's sons, said something to her husband about appealing to the Thunder Birds. He replied, "I'll leave it to them." There was a little light rain, but it soon stopped and fine weather continued during the rest of the ceremony. Everyone attributed this to the benevolence of the Thunder Birds although, so far as I know, no smoke offering was made.

CAUSATION AND COSMOLOGY

These anecdotes, besides illustrating occasions when spontaneous interaction with other than human persons may take place, also expose, as do the myths, Ojibwa notions about the causes of events. We must infer that their implicit theory of causation is *personalistic* since they do not actually speculate about such matters or attempt to articulate them in abstract form. However, since the Ojibwa do not have any concept of a natural world, it is hardly to be expected that in their thinking, any notion of impersonal causes, such as the regularities on which the formulation of natural law is based would arise. This does not mean, of course, that events in their world are considered as haphazard or unpredictable. But since an extended concept of persons occupies such a central position in their notion of being, it follows that the activities and interrelationships of such persons offer a satisfying foundation for explaining events. This foundation provides a base for interpreting interactions between other than human persons and between persons of this class and human beings and, following the same pattern, the influence of human beings upon each other.

Thus, the path Sun travels every day makes his behavior predictable—up to a point. But since Sun is a person, his habits may be interrupted by unexpected events, such as the setting of a snare on his trail by another person. In the myth the person who set the trap is also of the other than human class. In the anecdote about the interaction of the old men with Sun, however, his regular movements were influenced by persons of the human class.

Many personalistic explanations of past events are found in Ojibwa myths. It was *Wisekedjak,* for example, who through the exercise of his personal power, expanded the tiny bit of mud retrieved by Muskrat from the waters of the Great Deluge, until it reached the dimensions of the island earth of Ojibwa cosmography.[2] My friends at Pauingassi believed that the Thunder Birds, by withdrawing from that vicinity, made fair weather possible for their Wabano. Because of the beneficent attitude of these Thunder Birds towards man, these Indians found it difficult to understand the white man's ideas about thunder and lightning as natural phenomena. More than once I was specifically asked questions about this. Among other things they refused to believe that forest fires could be caused by lightning. Consequently, when a severe forest fire broke out just after World War II had begun in 1939, the personalistic pattern of explanation inclined the Ojibwa to believe a German spy had set the fire. The central question was: *Who* did it? *Somebody* must have been responsible. The Thunder Birds could not have caused the fire, and of course, no Indian could have started it. These Ojibwa remained firmly in the grip of a personalistic explanation of events.

When their cosmology is considered, however, it is interesting to discover that the creation of the world is not attributed to a person. They have no primordial creation myth. Occurrences in the myths are simply transformations in a world already in existence. This is one of the reasons why the vaguely conceived High God of the Ojibwa cosmos—the *Gitchi Manitu* of popular fame—is functionally so undefinable. His role is not that of a creator or even an *Urheber* (founder). Nevertheless, none of the evidence suggests that this High God was a direct consequence of contact with missionaries. This assertion is denied by the Ojibwa themselves, as it has been by scholars.[3] Descriptively, the problem turns upon the conceptualization of the attributes and functions of this being, who in most respects stands apart from the beings of the other than human class already discussed. The entities of this class are frequently figures in mythology, where they are given anthropomorphic, mammalian, or avian attributes. But since the High God does not appear in the myths, or in the shaking tent, or even in dreams, any kind of concrete visual image or clue to outward appearance is completely lacking. Since specific functional attributes are likewise lacking, it is extremely difficult to discuss the role of the High God with any surety. Writing more than a century ago, Henry R. Schoolcraft said that the Ojibwa attributed "benevolence and pity" to this "Great Transcendental Spirit." He also pointed out that man is not accountable to this being either "here or hereafter, for aberrations from virtue, good will, truth, or any form of moral right." The administration of affairs in the Ojibwa cosmos, added School-craft, is left to "demons and fiends in human form," that is, to the other than human persons I have described in more neutral and, I hope, accurate terms.

I suspect that as a result of the efforts of the missionaries, the High God may have come to assume a more central place than it held previously in the thinking of the Ojibwa as they came under the influence of Christianity. But the roles of the many other than human persons continued to be of pragmatic importance in meeting the hazards of life and in other traditional ways.

It may also be significant that the Ojibwa with whom I was acquainted had a name other than *k'tu manitu* (in Berens River speech) for the High God. The other name was *kadabendijiget,* meaning "owner" or "master." The same linguistic root occurs in the generic term applied to the "owners" of the natural species to which I have referred. This etymology suggests that in some general sense the High God was conceived of as the controller of the universe and for this reason very far removed from human persons. Furthermore, the "owners" of natural species are not major characters in the mythology, although they appear in the shaking tent. The imagery associated with them is derived in a vague way from the species they are reputed to control. In the shaking tent the "owner" of the Moose, for example, may call himself "Moose." But since the High God had no association with any empirical phenomena whatsoever, there was no point of departure for the projection of any parallel imagery in this case. It must be remembered, too, that since (as noted earlier in this chapter) there was no gender distinction in the Ojibwa language, the sex of this entity inevitably was left ambiguous. On the other hand, the conception of an enduring essence as the vital part of all beings of the person category made it possible for the belief in a being far removed from man, and distinct from other than human persons, to assume reality in terms of the basic metaphysical assumption held by the Ojibwa.

The temporal dimension of the Ojibwa world view is not systematically organized in any formal way. No fixed chronological order of cosmological events can be deduced from the myths. Events attributed to a past that cannot be connected with any known generation of human individuals are described as having taken place "long ago." Consequently, we are plunged into a bottomless temporal pit that lacks guideposts. Once we enter the mythological world of the Ojibwa, linear chronology loses all significance.

Nevertheless, certain episodes in the mythological narratives provide the basis for broad temporal inferences, particularly with respect to various kinds of changes that have occurred in the course of time. These were all the consequence of the activities of the other than human persons who were the chief protagonists in the myths. For the Ojibwa these changes are part of their folk history. One of these changes concerns the fate of the giant animals. Formerly, this earth was inhabited by many monster species, which are now represented only by smaller varieties of their kind. The myths present accounts of how some of the giant animals became extinct, for instance Great Mosquitoes, or how a familiar variety of some smaller animal, like snakes, came into existence. It was explained to me that the other than human beings of the past were sufficiently powerful to overcome these giant animals. But human beings of today would be constantly harassed if they had to live on earth with many creatures of this sort. A few varieties of these animals like Great Frogs and Snakes still survive, although there are very few left. Thus, the events in the myths involving the monster animals are thought of as belonging to a far distant past, "long ago" when the earth was "new."

Another temporal clue is afforded by the transformation in the appearances of certain animals by the anthropomorphic *Wisekedjak*. He made the kingfisher much prettier than this bird once was, shortened the tail of the muskrat, and gave the weasel a white coat in winter. Human beings, too, we may infer, were not always as they are now, either in appearance or knowledge. Until *Tcakábec* was scraped clean by his sister after being in the belly of a great fish, human beings were covered with hair. All women once had toothed vaginas, and until Wisekedjak, by accident, discovered the pleasure of sexual intercourse, no one knew about it.

The flood episode in one of the narratives of the Wisekedjak cycle also has important chronological implications since Wisekedjak and some of the animals, at least, must have inhabited an earlier land mass. But the Indians themselves do not appear to correlate such temporal implications in their mythological corpus as a whole. As a rule, the temporal sequences intrinsic to the events of each narrative are accepted without reference to other narratives. Events that are believed to have taken place "long ago" are not organized into any unified temporal scheme. But accounts of discrete changes are clearly brought out, and we get an impression of the immortal and stable nature of the other than human persons appearing in the myths. They were alive when the Ojibwa world was young, and they assisted the Indians then. They are still alive today and continue to aid mankind. The past and the present are part of a unified temporal whole because other than human persons, not even now grown old, remain in social interaction with succeeding generations of human persons in a cosmic society.

The earth on which human beings now live is thought to be flat. It is a great island, a conception that is supported rather than contradicted by Ojibwa who have been to school and have seen the Western Hemisphere depicted on maps. Under the earth is another land mass also inhabited by human beings. Since the Sun's trail leads over the earth during the day and under it during the night, there is daylight in the lower world when there is darkness on the earth and vice versa. The underworld was once visited by some Berens River Indians "long ago." They were out hunting, saw some strangers and followed them to the lower world. At first the people living there wanted to kill the Indians. But when they found the Ojibwa were so much like themselves, they spared their lives. Above the earth is Thunder Bird Land, a journey to which has already been referred to.

On the earth the homes of the Winds establish a basic directional schema for the Ojibwa. Direction is only partially abstracted from place. North is not an abstracted direction; it is the home of the North Wind. Other points of directional orientation are the North Star (another living being), and the movements of Sun. Directional orientation is therefore keyed to certain other than human persons in the Ojibwa cosmos. Furthermore, the structures used for ceremonies symbolize the cosmographical orientation of the Ojibwa, as does their pattern of dancing. The pavilion erected for the Wabano is always built on an east–west axis, as was that used for the Midewiwin in the past. The entrance faces the east. Dancing is always done "clockwise," as we call it, but the Ojibwa think of it in directional terms, that is, from east to south to west to north to east. This is likewise the order of birth of the four Winds as narrated in myth. In the ceremonial smoking of a pipe, too, the stem is turned in a clockwise direction with a slight pause when it faces in each direction. The symbolism of this act lies in the fact that turning the pipe in all directions allows other than human persons in the entire Ojibwa cosmos to receive a smoke offering.

THE LIVING AND THE DEAD

The Land of the Dead or, more literally, the Land of Ghosts (djibaiaking), is located in the south. This is probably the explanation of the north–south orientation of the body in a grave. The head is placed to the north, but the person is said to be facing the south. After death and a long hard journey, the vital part of a human being, including consciousness and personal memories, continues to exist in ghostly form in the most southerly part of the earth. This is a region where there is no winter season, no one has any trouble making a living, and no one is sick and needs medicine; so many aspects of life are different from that of human beings who remain alive. The deceased do not live as disembodied souls, however. They maintain a human form, although their bodies lie in a grave. This is why the term djibai used for them finds its closest translation as "ghost." After their journey south, human beings retain the dual aspect of all persons in the Ojibwa world; they still have an outward appearance and a vital enduring essence. A major difference,

Figure 11. Wabano pavilion at or near Little Grand Rapids. Although Hallowell did not record what signification was attached to the British flag, flag displays had been a feature of the fur trade in the region for 150 years (see, for example, Lytwyn 1986:35, 61), and Wabano leader John Duck felt his position enhanced by Hallowell's gift to him of an American flag bearing an eagle (Hallowell 1955:264).

however, between the living and the dead is epitomized by an incidental episode in an account of a human being who visited the Land of the Dead but managed to return. Shortly after arriving he was offered food by his parents whom he found there. But he could not eat it! In an account of a comparable journey reported from another Ojibwa group, there is a similar episode and reference is made to the "supremely selected food" of the dead, that is, decayed or phosphorescent wood. In both cases, the men who paid a visit to the Land of Ghosts could not eat because they were not dead [cf. Kohl 1985:217, 220–225].

Although spatially remote, the living and the dead are not completely cut off from one another; the latter are not forgotten by living persons. One old man, speaking of his Drum dance, referred again and again to the "old people down south," a euphemism for the ghostly dead, and said how much they enjoyed hearing the Indians up north beating the drum. And just as in the case of other than human persons, there are some occasions when the living and the dead communicate. In former times, food was always placed in a grave-house at the time of burial to provide the *djibai* with nourishment for the journey ahead. After burial, it was also the custom, which sometimes still happens, for relatives to place a little food at a grave from time to time. In the past, of course, the graves of deceased Ojibwa were much more scattered. When death occurred in the autumn and winter, individuals were buried wherever their relatives happened to be. There were no Christian

Figure 12. Graves at Little Grand Rapids in the 1940s, showing a variety of different structures and markers. Photograph by Cory Kilvert.

cemeteries as there are now on reserve land. So formerly, when Indians were paddling along some river or lake in the wilderness and noticed a grave, they might stop and go ashore, especially if they knew the person buried there. Finding some tea or tobacco in the grave-house, they might smoke or drink a cup of tea. To drink, eat, or smoke at a grave was equivalent to having a visit with the dead. As one informant put it, "If a person had been alive and well, he would have offered these things to you, if you had come to his wigwam. Even after he is dead, it makes him glad that you should stop and visit him." Thus, by leaving tea and tobacco at a grave-house from time to time, the kin of the deceased maintain a relationship with him, and this custom enables the spirit of the deceased to continue the tradition of hospitality.

Communication with the dead through the medium of food and tobacco is also carried out in another way. A little of both may be offered to the spirits of the dead by throwing them in the fire. I saw this done more than once. It is unnecessary to think of any particular person, nor need there be any special occasion for food offerings of this kind. This custom is no doubt connected with more formally organized Feasts of the Dead, references to which occur in the literature [Vecsey 1983:12, 71]. I obtained an account of one variant of such an annual ceremony held

*Figure 13. Drummers and drum used in the "Ghost (or Spirit of the Dead)
Dance" that originated from a dream revelation of Nämawin (Fair Wind), one of
the oldest Berens River men living in the 1930s (Hallowell 1955:165).*

north of the Berens River. In this ceremony the dead were represented by wooden
figures attached to a string inside a wigwam. When the drumming began, these
figures would dance. Across Lake Winnipeg at Jack Head there was another
ceremony held in the past in which *djibaiyak* were invoked and seen to pass through
the wigwam. I once attended a ceremony at Pauingassi (1933) in which the drum
was used as a means of communicating with the spirits of the dead. Said to have

Figure 14. Pavilion used in Nämawin's drum dance. Hallowell saw two per-formances of this dance: one at Pauingassi (Nämawin's home) in 1933, and one at Poplar Narrows in 1932, the pavilion for which is shown here. The Poplar Narrows people purchased from Nämawin the right to perform the dance in their community (Hallowell 1955:165–166; 402, n. 36).

originated locally, the ceremony seemed to combine in a novel way beliefs and practices more generally known, thus suggesting the kinds of variation that could have arisen in the past within the general framework of the Ojibwa world view. It expressed a strong culturally rooted motivation for keeping in touch with the spirits of the dead. There is some evidence that, occasionally at least, spirits of the dead could be of assistance to human beings in times of crisis, thus playing the role of so-called "guardian spirits," a role more generally performed by persons of the other than human class.

Reincarnation of the soul of a deceased person in a new human body is recognized as possible by the Ojibwa, although it does not happen very often. Certain specific clues are accepted, however, as evidence of actual reincarnation. One of these is the presence of a few gray hairs on the head of an infant. Another is the recall of memories from the prenatal period. A man whom I knew well once said to me:

Some people say that a child knows nothing when it is born. Four nights before I was born I knew that I would be born. My mind was as clear when I was born as it is now. I saw my father and mother, and I knew who they were. I knew the things an Indian uses, their names and what they were good for—an axe, a gun, a knife. I used to tell this to my father and he said: "Long ago the Indians used to be like that, but the ones that came after them were different." I have asked children about this, but there is only one of them who remembers when he was in his mother's womb. People said to me: "You are one of those old people who died long ago and were born a second time."

But this old man did not make this claim to me.

Another clue to reincarnation is when infants cry and babble until someone recognizes the name they are trying to articulate so hard in order to establish their personal identity. I discovered in my genealogies that the occurrence of identical names, sometimes more than a generation apart, could be explained in every case by reincarnation. Unfortunately none of these persons were alive at the time, so I could not interview any of them.

Although the ghostly spirits of the dead do not occupy a central position in the Ojibwa world view and are not the objects of any organized cult, in their relations to living human beings they show some coalescence, conceptually and functionally, with other than human persons. In the last analysis, the inescapable fact is that the vital part of man is as immortal as the equivalent essence of other than human persons. In the perspective of Ojibwa cosmology, persons of both classes belong to the category of ancient and enduring beings because the world of Being itself has no beginning and no end, despite minor transformation in outward appearance. This conceptualization of the world structures the behavioral environment in which succeeding generations of living Ojibwa have to adjust themselves in relation to each other and to the greater society in which they participate. When Ojibwa *behave* consistently with their beliefs about the world, they assert the psychological realities of their behavioral environment and the traditional values of their culture. The sociopsychological realities that emerge from this fact are as important for understanding the personality structure of individuals as they are for understanding how the sociocultural system of the Ojibwa maintains itself as an integrating whole.

EDITOR'S NOTES

1. Much of the material in this chapter is a recasting of the analysis in one of Hallowell's best known essays, "Ojibwa Ontology, Behavior and World View," first published in 1960 and reprinted as Chapter 9 in Hallowell 1976. Readers interested in consulting a more extensive and fully documented overview of the subjects presented here are referred to that important article.

2. For a Cree example of this myth and for a broad overview of these creation and flood motifs among Algonquian people, see Brown and Brightman 1988:47–48, 130–132.

3. Debates on the aboriginality (and definition) of a High God continue. See, for example, Vecsey 1983:80–82; Long 1986:173–175; and Brown and Brightman 1988:107–108.

6 / Religion, Moral Conduct, and Personality

A CULTURALLY CONSTITUTED WORLD

The preceding chapter outlined the central features of an outlook upon the world that gives the *actors* in the Ojibwa sociocultural system their basic cognitive orientation and structures their behavioral environment. In Robert Redfield's words, world view

> attends especially to the way a man, in a particular society, sees himself in relation to all else. It is the properties of existence as distinguished from and related to the self. It is, in short, a man's idea of the universe. It is that organization of ideas which answers to a man the questions: Where am I? Among what do I move? What are my relations to these things? . . . Self is the axis of world view [Redfield 1952:30].

Thus, beliefs about the nature of their world and the position they occupy in it as persons become integral components, for the Ojibwa, of perceiving, remembering, imagining, judging, and reasoning. Succeeding generations of Ojibwa have learned to become cognizant, in whole or in part, of their culturally constituted world. They have had to adjust themselves to each other and to the persons of the greater cosmic society in which they believe themselves to be participants, in the terms set by their tradition. Insofar as individuals have been motivated to act in accordance with the premises of their world view, the psychological realities of their behavioral environment and the values and goals of their culture have been unconsciously asserted. The sociopsychological realities arising from this fact are as important for understanding the distinctive features of the personality structure of individuals as they are for understanding how the sociocultural system of the Ojibwa has maintained its continuity with the past, as well as having changed under the influence of historical events.

From the point of view of Ojibwa individuals the primary psychological fact to be emphasized is that their world view engenders an attitude of dependence upon persons of the other than human class. It is these other than humans who take pity on *anishinabek* and recognize their needs and desires. To achieve culturally defined goals, human beings require knowledge and power from persons of this class that cannot be obtained from any other source. Little can be accomplished by their own inherent capabilities. Indeed, it may be said that neither myth, tale, nor tradition represented a human being as making any discovery, bringing about any change, or achieving any status or influence unaided by other than human persons. There are no incentives to individualistic invention or creativity in Ojibwa culture. Even though myths exhibit minor variations and may be borrowed and adapted from elsewhere [Hallowell 1939], they are repeated, not invented. The same major characters appear because myths are considered to be "true" stories about past events. Consequently, there is no category of oral literature that is recognized as fiction, nor any motivation to create it. The Ojibwa have songs, but for the most part, these too are not human creations. They are said to be derived from contacts with other than human persons. Human beings, then, from birth to death, have constant need of the assistance of other than human beings. This is why even the personal identity of all Ojibwa individuals was formerly signaled in a traditional naming ceremony in which a grandparent bestowed some of the power, previously derived from other than human sources, upon a newborn child.

Faith in the power of other than human persons, trust in the essential help they can offer human beings, and dependence upon them in order to achieve a good life define the psychological core of Ojibwa religion when considered in the framework of their world view. Among these Indians religion cannot be comprehended in terms of a natural–supernatural dichotomy of being because these categories are inseparable in Ojibwa thought. It cannot be understood by simply referring to a belief in "spiritual beings," since beings of this order are essentially similar in their major characteristics to human persons. Nor do terms such as prayer, sacrifice, and worship, as applied to Ojibwa activities, convey a meaning that illuminates key features of their religious behavior. Even a consideration of their ceremonies does not, in itself, enable us to penetrate the heart of Ojibwa religion. The core of their religion lies in the characteristic forms taken by the interpersonal relations they seek to maintain between themselves and other than human beings. This religious core manifests itself in widely ramified contexts, rather than being sharply focused in highly organized institutions or ceremonies. Based upon the differences believed to exist between the inherent power possessed by man and by "our grandfathers," Ojibwa religion in its primary emphasis is closely linked with the fundamental pragmatic values of Ojibwa culture. The religious "path" they follow is chosen because it leads to the enhancement of the limited capabilities of human persons. Religious behavior meets the needs defined by the image of themselves reflected in their world view. Because of these needs, the existence of other than human persons can never be ignored. Since these beings are so omnipresent, religious behavior is difficult if not impossible to compartmentalize; it emerges in contexts where it may seem quite incidental from the standpoint of an outsider. A bit of tobacco left in a tiny hole when a medicinal plant is gathered, the response Fair Wind made when he thought a Thunder Bird had spoken to him, the hanging of a skull of a slain animal in the branch of a tree; all these offer behavioral testimony of an awareness of the existence of other than human persons and man's dependence on them.

In my own experience I was inclined at first, as others have done, to distinguish Ojibwa dances from those ceremonies where prolonged singing, beating the drum, and periodic dancing occurred, and whose religious orientation appeared to be obvious. But I soon discovered that any facile distinction between the secular and the sacred from the Ojibwa point of view was not so easy to draw. If I missed the first few minutes of what I thought might be a purely secular "dance," I also missed a smoke offering to "our grandfathers." Yet, after this offering was made, nothing took place that was comparable to a ceremonial affair like the Wabano. The Wabano was more ostensibly linked with man's relations with other than human beings, but this link was not omitted in the dance.

SEEKING THE GOOD LIFE

Thus, Ojibwa religious behavior, comprehensively viewed, can be identified as any activity by an individual or a group of individuals that helps to promote a good life for human beings by making explicit recognition, direct or indirect, of man's faith in and dependence upon other than human persons. For this reason as we shall see, religion is also related to what is considered good conduct, although unlike Christianity, no linkage is made with any prospect of reward or punishment in the Land of the Dead. Religious behavior, too, is linked psychologically with the characterological traits of individuals, stemming directly from interpersonal relations with other than human beings. And since behavioral conformity is necessarily linked with the values and norms of the Ojibwa sociocultural system, religious behavior contributes to the maintenance of that system.

Human beings may benefit, both indirectly and directly, from the superior knowledge and power possessed by other than human persons. The naming ceremony is an example of benefits conveyed indirectly. A child's life is enhanced by "blessings" bestowed originally upon an older person. The services institutionalized in a shaking tent performance are another example. It is only the conjurer himself who has directly obtained the power to invoke other than human persons so that they can help meet the needs of human beings. Humans must therefore appeal to the conjurer for assistance, knowing that the validity of his services derives from the knowledge and power he has received directly from other than human sources. For the Ojibwa, all the values implicit in a life free from hunger, illness, and misfortune are in part contingent upon help that in various forms comes indirectly or directly from other than human persons. The Good Life is expressed by the term *pimädazi-win,* which is often articulated in ceremonies when a tobacco offering is made by turning a pipe in all directions of the cosmos. The High God may sometimes be mentioned by name, a consequence, perhaps, of Christian influence. In one ceremonial speech that I heard, *Manitu* was referred to as the "owner of everything" and the one who "knows what we need." But the same speaker also said that "blessings" might be expected from other than human beings in "the North, South, East, and West" and that thanks must be given for *pimädaziwin* (Life).

Although the cooperation of human beings and one's own personal efforts are recognized as necessary for the achievement of the Good Life, the help of other than human persons cannot be omitted. Generally speaking, it is only in the purely technological sphere—the tanning of skins, the making of moccasins and birchbark canoes, the shaping of articles of wood such as snowshoes—that human beings can learn all they need to know from other human beings. In hunting, although there is plenty to learn about the habits of animals, how to handle weapons, how to bait a deadfall, or set a trap, this is not enough. The cooperation of the "owners" of the various species is also required since these entities control the animals.

Figure 15. Nämawin (Fair Wind), also known as John Owen, with snowy owl (?) wing. He died in 1944 at the age of 93 (information courtesy of Gary Buti-kofer).

Cures for illness, as among other peoples, are also important among the Ojibwa. Knowledge of the reputed medicinal properties of some plants is handed down in an empirically based tradition and constitutes a native pharmacopoeia. This body of materia medica alone, however, is not considered adequate for curing all kinds of sickness. Medicine men of several different varieties achieve preeminence from the fact that they have obtained special skills from other than human sources, whose

Figure 16. John Duck and his Wabano pavilion, Little Grand Rapids.

help is essential for curing more serious kinds of human illness. Confidence in the skill of these men and the prestige they enjoy rest upon the belief that they have acquired the knowledge they possess through direct contact with other than human persons. The same is true of the men who are the leaders of the Wabano, which, since the disappearance of the Midewiwin, has proliferated. It includes curing functions, and dancing in the Wabano pavilion is considered to be therapeutic. In this case as in others, persons of the other than human class are never forgotten, so that if we bear in mind the pragmatic focus of Ojibwa religion, participation in Wabano ceremonies is another example of the relationship between human and other than human persons.

DREAMS AND POWER

The most significant and vital contact between Ojibwa individuals and their other than human "grandfathers" can occur only in one kind of context—the dream state. It is only through this direct and intimate contact that individuals receive the personal benefits so important to them, even though the benefits acquired may become socially significant where shared with their fellow men. Direct contact with other than human persons is a source of power, intangible except in the manner in which it is used and the prestige that accrues from its possession. Individuals can enhance their opportunities for the Good Life through direct contact with other than human beings in dreams, and may at the same time achieve a high status in Ojibwa society by demonstrations of their power. In a wider frame of reference dream experiences are a vital aspect of the religious orientation of the Ojibwa, if belief systems are considered as having psychological functions.

It is not surprising, then, that the literature on the Ojibwa for more than a century and a half has often referred to the special interest the Ojibwa manifest in dreams. It has been said that they have great faith in or are dependent upon their dreams; that they "go to school in dreams"; that good dreaming is necessary before undertaking important enterprises, and that "guardian spirits" are acquired in dreams. It is necessary to emphasize, however, that it is not the dreaming itself that is significant, but rather the integral association in the Ojibwa mind between the nature of persons, as postulated in their world view, and the vivid imagery and hallucinatory quality of dreams. In this context it is not difficult to understand why the most intimate contacts between human beings and other than human persons can only occur in dreams.

The Ojibwa, in short, interpret the manifest content of dreams as experiences of the self, continuous in time and space with those of waking life. For them, the vital, enduring part of a human being can undergo all sorts of experiences while the body—the outer shell—lies quiet and inert in sleep. For us dream images are recognized as self-related when their content is recalled, but they are not integrated with our personal experiences when awake. Our world of dreams is usually considered to be a world of unreality and fantasy that contrasts with perceptually sensed experience when awake. For the Ojibwa no such sharp dichotomy exists, although they do not confuse waking life with sleep. What they do accept is the equivalence of all experience known to the self so far as memory, reflective thought, and conduct are concerned. This equivalence is possible because for them, the body is not a necessary condition for experience; the locus of personal identity and experience is the soul, which may become detached from the body. When a person is asleep, anyone can see that his body is there but you can't tell whether his soul is there or not.

I already have mentioned that the "souls" of living persons, when they are asleep, may be brought into the shaking tent where they may be heard speaking. I was told about one seance in which the conjurer said, "I'm calling for the man from Lac Seul." Shortly afterwards there was a thump indicating a new arrival in the tent, followed by a strange voice saying, "I was sleeping, but I heard you calling me." This was the soul of a noted Lac Seul conjurer. People in the audience asked for news and received replies to questions. Then the visiting conjurer sang a song and departed for his home 200 miles away. Thus, the soul of a sleeping person has a mobility in space far beyond that which is possible for his body either in waking life or when asleep. Consequently, the hallucinatory images of dreams may be interpreted as the personal experiences of a detached soul in sleep. When recalled, dreams can be connected in various ways with other life experiences of the dreamer.

My friend, William Berens, for example, told me of a dream he had when he was about 16 years old. One winter night after he had gone to sleep, he saw a young man approaching the camp from the north:

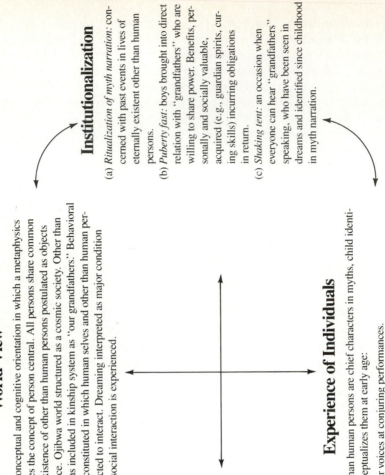

Institutionalization

(a) *Ritualization of myth narration*: concerned with past events in lives of eternally existent other than human persons.

(b) *Puberty fast*: boys brought into direct relation with "grandfathers" who are willing to share power. Benefits, personally and socially valuable, acquired (e.g., guardian spirits, curing skills) incurring obligations in return.

(c) *Shaking tent*: an occasion when everyone can hear "grandfathers" speaking, who have been seen in dreams and identified since childhood in myth narration.

World View

Embodies a conceptual and cognitive orientation in which a metaphysics of being makes the concept of person central. All persons share common properties. Existence of other than human persons postulated as objects in cosmic space. Ojibwa world structured as a cosmic society. Other than human persons included in kinship system as "our grandfathers." Behavioral environment constituted in which human selves and other than human persons are expected to interact. Dreaming interpreted as major condition under which social interaction is experienced.

Experience of Individuals

Since other than human persons are chief characters in myths, child identifies and conceptualizes them at early age:

Hears their voices at conjuring performances.

Has direct personal contact with these entities in dreams.

Operation of System

Socialization of child: acquisition of belief system, values, and goals. *Social control* centered in responsibility for conduct, i.e., rights and obligations that involve relations with both classes of persons. *Illness* interpreted as punishment for transgression of socially sanctioned obligations. Reflection on past conduct, guilt, confession of wrongdoing in order to recover.

Figure 17. The role of dreams in the Ojibwa sociocultural system.

He came and stood at my feet as I lay sleeping. "You are wanted over there," he said, motioning with his lips towards the north. I got up and started off with him. I found that we were traveling through the air, not along the ground. I looked down and saw a river ahead of us and just one *pi'kogan* [conical tipi]. I could see the kind of trees growing there. There were lots of very straight jackpine on the north side of the river. Now we came down to the ground near another kind of tent. I walked into it. There I saw a man I knew in the center. I could see no end to the tent, it stretched out as far as I could see and it was full of all kinds of people. I knew then that I was inside a conjuring tent. "I'm going out," I said. But the old man said: "No! You can't go." Then I saw my own head rolling about and the people in the lodge were trying to catch it. I thought to myself, if only I can catch my head everything will be all right. So I tried to grab it when it rolled near me. Finally I caught it. As soon as I got hold of it I could see my way and I left. Then I woke up.

William Berens was sick for a few days after he dreamed this, but he recovered. He believed, and so did his father, that a conjurer whose son he had insulted had tried to kill him but had failed.[1]

DREAM VISITORS AND FASTING

If dreams are interpreted as experiences of the self, it is during sleep, when the soul of a human being can easily become free from its bodily envelope, that direct personal contacts with other than human persons occur. Under certain circumstances other than human grandfathers visit their human grandchildren. In this context they are often referred to as "dream visitors," *pawáganak*. On such occasions it is the vital part of human beings (*òtcatcákwin*) that comes into direct communication with the enduring essence of other than human persons. Reference already has been made to other occasions when human beings become aware of the presence of other than humans as, for example, in the shaking tent. But on these public occasions intimate person-to-person communication is not possible. It is only in the dream state that "blessings" in the form of knowledge and power are received from other than human sources. Dream experiences of this kind were not only private; it was forbidden to talk about them except under the most unusual circumstances. These were the most significant dream experiences of all.

From the age of six years onward, Ojibwa children of both sexes were encouraged to dream. The dreaming of boys, however, was given special emphasis through the institutionalization of a prepuberty fast, which, although it had almost died out at the time of my investigations, was formerly undertaken by every boy. It was in this way that boys between the ages of 10 and 14 years were given an opportunity to secure "blessings" from direct personal contact with their other than human grandfathers. It was assumed that these "grandfathers," recognizing the immaturity of their human grandsons, were willing to share their superior power and knowledge with them so that they might have the Good Life. They took "pity" on the boys, visited them during their fasting period, and became their tutelaries, or "guardian spirits." For the boys, the fast was a lonely vigil lasting a week or more, spent out in the forest in the spring. The father, stepfather, or human grandfather of a boy built a sort of platform for him in a tree (a nest, or *wázisan*). The faster was forbidden to descend to the ground, except for a little water perhaps and to urinate and defecate. The boy had to be sexually "pure" or the fast was useless. Even less intimate relations with girls and women were avoided immediately before and after the fast, which signaled both the psychological and social identification of boys with mature members of their own sex. For several days before departing the boy slept in the "cleanest" place in the dwelling, that is, towards the rear, in the area reserved for the men. Before this he had slept near the front, near his mother and other prepubertal children. During the fasting period the boy's father or grandfather might sing and drum to communicate with his own other than human tutelaries and to invoke help on behalf of the dreamer. The faster usually returned to camp shortly after daybreak. He hid in the bushes and signaled his presence by a whistle or call familiar to his father, who went to him immediately and accompanied him to the camp. In this way a boy avoided meeting a woman first, since this would endanger his "blessings."

The prepuberty fast thus epitomized the dichotomy between the characteristic roles that men were expected to play in the sociocultural system of the Ojibwa and those of women. It was the prerogative of the males to engage in all the activities that required the greatest assistance from and closest cooperation with other than human persons, who like themselves were males. The men were the hunters, curers, conjurers, the leaders of ceremonies such as the Wabano and, in the past, of the Midewiwin. It was in the prepuberty fast that boys, besides receiving personal benefits, were invested with power and skills that, when exercised in their mature years, benefited their community. Although women also had "dream visitors" and in exceptional cases might even play some of the same roles as men after menopause, any "blessings" they received had only a personal significance. This was why there was no necessity for institutionalized dreaming for girls. The functioning of the sociocultural system of the Ojibwa depended in part upon the recruitment of the services of men in roles, such as curing, which had a social significance. The only legitimate validation of these roles was derived from direct contact with other than human persons in dreams. The personal acquisition of "guardian spirits" served to engender confidence in meeting the vicissitudes of life for both sexes. But in this patri-centered culture, the dream fast was the most crucial experience of a man's life. The personal relations he established with his "dream visitors" determined a great deal of his destiny as an individual. Every boy met the "persons" on whom he could most firmly depend in time of need, and a few acquired exceptional skills and powers that carried the greatest prestige in Ojibwa society. To a man, relations with other than human persons were an enduring source of his inner security. The grandfather of one of my informants said to him: "You will have a long and good life if you dream well."

DREAM EXPERIENCES AND TEACHINGS

It appears that no information from any Ojibwa group on the content of fasters' dreams has ever been obtained immediately or even soon after the fast itself. All dreams of this type on record were told by acculturated adults in later life and in some cases were filtered through another person. As a matter of fact, since recounting experiences in a dream fast violated an obligation to an other than human person and led to the loss of any "blessings" obtained, no investigator could have obtained such information from a subject at the period when institutionalized dreaming for boys was flourishing.

Nevertheless, some fragments of such experiences came to my attention. While one boy was fasting, a "dream visitor" appeared to him in human form. But the faster did not know his identity. Later, this being said: "Grandchild, I think you are strong enough to go with me now." Then this *pawágan* began dancing. As he danced he turned into what looked like a golden eagle. It became apparent to the boy then that this must be the "owner" of this species of bird. Glancing down at his own body, the dreamer noticed it was covered with feathers. The "eagle" spread its wings and flew off towards the south. The dreamer then spread his wings and followed. In this dream we find the instability of outward form in both human and other than human persons succinctly dramatized. Individuals of both categories underwent metamorphosis. In later life the boy would recall that in his dream fast he became transformed into a bird. This does not imply that at any time in the future the boy could transform himself at will into a golden eagle, but he learned by personal experience that such a metamorphosis is possible for a human being. In this instance, the dream does not inform us whether the boy's "blessings" included the power of self-transformation.

Among the Berens River Ojibwa it was possible to learn some details about the basic patterns and kinds of dream experiences that occurred in the traditional dream fast because some of the skills formerly validated by such experiences still persisted, despite the decline of institutionalized dreaming for all prepubertal boys. The vital importance these skills had for the Ojibwa, despite a long period of acculturation, was evident. Such specialized curing procedures, for instance, as the removal of lethal objects projected magically into a person's body, the use of medicine that could be obtained from *memengwéciwak,* and the practice of conjuring by means of the shaking tent still flourished to some extent. These skills still required dream validation. But this validation by other than human persons, although required, had become acceptable even if it did not occur in a prepuberty dream fast. In other words, the "owners" or "bosses" of these skills, equivalent to the "masters" of the animal species, were still believed to exist, and human beings could still come into direct contact with them in dreams. I was told, for example, that four visits from the "master of conjuring" are necessary in order to become fully instructed. This "master" lives in the western part of the Ojibwa cosmos but not on the earth. Even details about the kind of wood to be selected for the poles of the shaking tent are communicated. The "master" also designates the "moon" (month) in which a man's first conjuring performance must take place. He is also told not to conjure too frequently or just for fun. There must be a real need for his services.

The traditional interpretation of dream experiences remained so persistent that even highly acculturated Indians like my friend William Berens recalled dreams that clearly illuminated the cultural patterning of dreams associated with the old prepuberty fast. He told me that one dream would have enabled him to become a *manäo* like his great-grandfather, if he had so desired. A doctor of this kind dispenses medicine obtained directly from *memengwéciwak*. William Berens dreamed he was out hunting and met one of these other than human persons.

> I claimed a high rock to have a look across the lake. I thought I might sight a moose or some ducks. When I glanced down towards the water's edge again, I saw a man standing by the rock. He was leaning on his paddle. A canoe was drawn up to the shore and in the stern sat a woman. In front of her rested a cradleboard with a baby in it. Over the baby's face was a piece of green mosquito netting [exactly the same as Indian women use for the same purpose]. The man was a stranger to me but I went up to him. I noticed that he hung his head in a strange way. He said, "You are the first human being ever to see me. I want you to come and visit me." So I jumped into his canoe. When I looked down I noticed that it was all of one piece. There were no ribs or anything of the sort, and there was no bark covering. I do not know what it was made of.
>
> On the northwest side of the lake there was a very high steep rock. The man headed directly for this rock. With one stroke of the paddle we were across the lake. The man threw his paddle down as we landed on a flat shelf of rock almost level with the water. Behind this the rest of the rock rose steeply before us. But when his paddle touched the rock this part opened up. He pulled the canoe in and we entered a room in the rock. It was not dark there, although I could see no holes to let in any light. Before I sat down, the man said, "See, there is my father and my mother." The hair of those old people was as white as a rabbitskin. I could not see a single black hair on their heads. After I had seated myself I had a chance to look around. I was amazed at all the articles I saw in the room—guns, knives, pans, and other trade goods. Even the clothing these people wore must have come from a store. Yet I never remembered having seen this man at a trading post. I thought I would ask him, so I said, "You told me that I was the first human being you had seen. Where, then, did you buy all of these articles I see?" To this he replied, "Have you never heard people talking about *pagiticigan* [offerings]? These articles were given to us. That is how we got them." Then he took me into another room and told me to look around. I saw the meat of all kinds of animals—moose, caribou, deer, ducks. I thought to myself, this man must be a wonderful hunter if he has been able to store up all this meat. I thought it very strange that this man had never met any other Indians in all his travels. Of course, I did not know that I was dreaming. Everything was the same as I had seen it with my eyes open. When I was ready to go I got up and shook hands with the man. He said, "Anytime that you wish to see me, this is the place where you will find me." He did not offer to open the door for me so I knew that I had to try and do this myself. I threw all the power of my mind into opening it and the rock lifted up. Then I woke up and knew that it was a dream.

William Berens added that some time later when he was awake and out hunting, he recognized the exact spot he had visited in his dream. He said he could have gone back there at any time and obtained the special kind of medicine for which the *memengwéciwak* are famous. This dream also reflects the conceptual and empirical unity of the spatiotemporal world of the Ojibwa and why it is possible for individuals to integrate *all* self-related experience in terms of it; any dichotomy between experiences when awake and those undergone in sleep is unnecessary.

The Ojibwa clearly recognize and take for granted that the knowledge and power acquired by human beings from other than human persons vary greatly. One man may acquire a great many more "guardian spirits" than another, and the "blessings" of one person may differ greatly from those of another. Only a few individuals acquire exceptional powers. In these cases no sharp line divides human from other than human persons. A particular man, for example, may be able to exercise a variety of specialized curing skills; he may be the leader of a Wabano and also a conjurer. Such a man may have sufficient power to make his fellow men sick or to kill them as well as cure them. Exceptional men may be able to make inanimate objects behave as if they were animate. They may be able to transform ashes into gunpowder, or a handful of goose feathers into birds or insects. In such displays of power they become elevated to the same level as other than human persons. We can, in fact, find comparable episodes in the myths. Thus, despite the inherent power attributed to other than human persons and man's acknowledged dependence on them, there is an intergradation in the power hierarchy of the Ojibwa world. Some human beings seem to have been able to closely approach, if not rival, other than human persons in power. This is another factor that unifies the cosmic society of the Ojibwa rather than sharply dividing the participants in it.

DREAMING AND THE MORAL ORDER

Above all, the other than human grandfathers of the Ojibwa world perhaps are sensed as persons because in communication with them in dreams, human beings discover that they act as participants in the same moral order as themselves. Indeed, this is implicit in the fact that all persons of the other than human class are willing to share their knowledge and power with their human grandchildren. This is the assumption on which the prepuberty fast for boys is based as well as the general interpretation of certain kinds of dream experiences as being the occasion of visits form other than human persons. For the obligation to share what one has with others is one of the central values of Ojibwa social organization and economic life. Emphasis is laid upon egalitarian values that serve to distribute goods and services equally in an economy where traditionally there was no market.

These values are still expressed through sharing, borrowing, and mutual exchange. They operate in the winter hunting groups and among the members of the dwelling clusters in the summer settlements. Dependence upon hunting and fishing for a living is precarious at best. Hunger is the silent enemy. Even though a hunter may exercise his best technical skills and treat the animals he kills properly, it is impossible to accumulate food for the inevitable rainy day. Consequently, a reciprocal principle is operative. If I have more than I need today I share it with you, because I know that you, in turn, will share what you have with me tomorrow. In Ojibwa culture there are no incentives for individuals to try and surpass their fellows in the accumulation of material goods. On the contrary, no one is expected to have much more than anyone else except temporarily. Any accumulation of goods is considered to be evidence of personal greediness, which is abhorred.

It is of particular interest, then, to observe that egalitarian values also apply to the relations between human persons and their other than human grandfathers. From the Ojibwa point of view "our grandfathers" have more power than they need. This is why they are expected to share it. It is even more significant, however, that in sharing it, egalitarian values are also recognized by other than human persons.

Greediness in the acquisition of power is as much discountenanced by them as in the hoarding of material goods of their "grandchildren."

I was once told about the dream fast of a boy who was not satisfied with his initial "blessing." He wanted to dream of all the leaves of all the trees in the world so that absolutely nothing would be hidden from him. This was considered greedy; although the *pawágan* who appeared in his dream granted his desire, the boy was told, "as soon as the leaves start to fall you'll get sick, and when all the leaves drop to the ground, that will be the end of your life." Overfasting is considered as greedy as hoarding. It violates a basic moral value of the cosmic society of the Ojibwa.

BLESSINGS, ILLNESS, AND CONFESSION

The "blessings" obtained from other than human persons were never free gifts. Benefits involved reciprocal moral obligations on the part of the recipient. In principal, the relationship paralleled social interaction between human beings where rights and duties were operative. The full benefit of the power and knowledge obtained from other than human persons was always contingent upon the fulfillment of obligations that took a variety of forms. In cases where the "owners" of animal species dispensed benefits, there was often a food taboo. One man was forbidden to kill or eat porcupine by the "owner" of the porcupines. In another case a man was commanded to wear the kind of headgear attributed to a character in mythology who had blessed him in a dream. Another man was forbidden to speak to or to have sexual intercourse with his wife for a defined period after marriage. Such obligations are never talked about because a general taboo is directed against any reference to the relations of a man and his "dream visitors," except in the most allusive manner or under unusual circumstances. The prohibition upon the narration of myths in summer, because this is not the proper time to talk about "our grandfathers," is of the same order.

Consequently, the observance of the personal taboos imposed by other than human persons often requires the firmest self-discipline, especially when it means behaving in ways that are not always intelligible to others yet cannot be explained to them. The man who was forbidden to sleep with his wife or even to talk to her did not succeed in fulfilling his obligation. She did not understand his conduct and could not tolerate it. She left him after one winter of married life. He married again and this time he broke the taboo. But now he suffered misfortune. One of his children became sick and died; later his new wife died. He married a third time and the same thing happened. It was useless for him to expect *pimädaziwin*. He had received a "blessing," but he had not been able to exercise sufficient self-control to benefit by it.

Personal food taboos are also interpreted so rigidly that inadvertent or unconscious violations do not modify the penalty for their infraction. The linquistic term for any infraction of the commands of other than human persons literally means, "failure to observe an obligation earnestly entered into." Failure to follow the command of an other than human being means not simply the loss of the benefits that might accrue from a personal "blessing"; nonfulfillment of the conditions that it entails violates a moral obligation that is subject to the same penalty as that applied to deviation from expected conduct in the interpersonal relations of human beings. Such failure is one variety of "bad conduct," that is, behavior that fails to conform with normative standards of conduct. The inevitable penalty for all "bad conduct" is serious illness. "Because a person does bad things, that is where sickness starts," is the way one informant phrased it. Bad conduct, the Ojibwa say, "will keep following you"; sooner or later you will suffer because of it. And besides this your children, or perhaps your wife, may suffer too by becoming sick or even dying. Thus, causes of illness are sought by the Ojibwa within their web of interpersonal relations, both human and cosmic. This causality is consistent with a world view in which the interrelation of *persons* is of paramount importance. This is likewise the setting in which the fear of becoming seriously ill functions as the major social sanction in the Ojibwa sociocultural system.

This traditional attitude towards illness gives the lives of the Ojibwa a hypo-chondriacal coloring[2] which has persisted even among more acculturated groups. Robert Ritzenthaler [1953], who studied reservation Ojibwa (Chippewa) in Wisconsin, was struck by "the inordinate amount of attention" they gave to health and healing. It also may be pointed out that although some plant medicines may have been of value in the cure of minor ailments,[3] the fact remains that Ojibwa knowledge of the actual causes of disease fell far below the level of their knowledge of the habits of animals and the efficiency of their technological equipment, simple though it was. If hunger may be called their "silent enemy," disease was a latent threat to *pimädaziwin* that they were less well prepared to meet. Although the absence in aboriginal days of such infectious diseases as measles, smallpox, and syphilis made disease problems less acute than after European contact, I believe it is fair to say that the Ojibwa system of medicine could hardly have contributed much to their biological survival and ecological adaptation. If on the other hand, we consider the functioning of their sociocultural system in relation to their interpretation of the significance of illness, we can see that their *attitude* towards disease is more important than the cure of it. The association of illness with punishment and the anxiety that this engendered introduced the psychosomatic factors necessary for the functioning of the major negative sanctions on Ojibwa behavior.

Correlated with this system of sanctions was the absence of any organized superordinate modes of social control. There was no council of elders or any forum in which judgment could be passed upon the conduct of adults. No institutionalized means existed for the public adjudication of disputes or conflicts of any kind. There was no traditional way in which publicly sanctioned punishment could be initiated in cases of incest, murder, or any other offense by a central authority. Prior to the relations of the Northern Ojibwa with the Dominion government and their familiarity with the Royal Canadian Mounted Police, institutionalized forms of penal sanctions were unknown to them. In their own cultural tradition, organized sanctions of this kind had no native roots. This is why chiefs, even since Treaty 5, have had so little local influence and have played no vital role in social control. Social control in the Ojibwa sociocultural system belonged to a type that operated through psychological mechanisms. Motivations that reinforced normative conduct were closely linked with ego and superego functioning, which compelled individuals to assume responsibility for their own moral conduct through inner control, rather than by responding to organized sanctions imposed from without. This pattern involved sensitivity to feelings of guilt and readiness to accept blame for one's own behavior. This is why any serious illness aroused anxiety; it pointed directly to some sort of bad conduct. Consequently, illness had more than a personal significance; it was a clear indication that there had been some departure from the accepted values that served to channel the relations of human beings with each other, as well as with other than human persons.

The seriousness of the failure to fulfil obligations to other than human persons is exemplified in the firm belief that the sickness that inevitably follows cannot be cured. Other than human persons have done what they could for me; they have shared their power with me. If I have been unable to do my part, it is my own fault. I only have myself to blame. It is for this reason that other than human persons are not conceived of as punishing figures, playing an authoritative role in any way comparable to a human father. If any analogy is made, their role is, in fact, much like that of "grandfathers" in the kinship structure. Thus, the severity of the penalty for failure to fulfil obligations to other than human persons typifies the necessity on the part of human beings of learning to accept responsibility for one's own conduct without any threat from authoritative figures of any kind.

On the other hand, the fact should not be overlooked that when the "blessings" obtained from other than human sources do eventuate in some public service, everyone can be assured that all the conditions have been met that guarantee that the powers of a medicine man or conjurer are genuine. This guarantee reinforces the prestige of these men. Since they must be paid well for their services, it is necessary that they inspire confidence in their clients. Understandably, therefore, it is shocking to the Ojibwa when occasionally a healer is discovered to be a charlatan. He has been deceiving his public; he has been practicing medicine without a "license," that is, without authentic dream experiences. Deception of this kind also falls under a disease sanction. A conjurer whom I heard about began to suffer from acute insomnia and then developed a phobia. He found that he could not go into the woods alone, even for a few hundred yards. One can readily understand how abnormal this kind of phobia was in a hunter. He was given medicine but to no avail. Finally he confessed his deceit and subsequently recovered. This case documents in concrete form how illness operates as a penalty for the violation of the mores of Ojibwa society. It also points to confession as the essential step towards recovery in instances where some kind of bad conduct is believed to be the cause of illness.

Ojibwa medicine men have a dual role to play. If materia medica fails and illness is prolonged, or if sickness takes the form of what we would classify as nervous or mental disorder, as in the case mentioned, the doctor has to probe for the "moral" cause of the trouble. The patient has to be stimulated to reflect upon his own past conduct. As may easily be imagined, feelings of guilt become particularly acute when children too young to be penalized for their own bad conduct may be suffering because of misdeeds of their parents. Thus, whether I become ill or my children do, the question arises: What have *I* done that was wrong? With the help of a doctor, I have to answer this question concretely. I have to think about my relations with other persons, both human and other than human. I have to identify the bad conduct that has followed me, even if it is necessary to go back to my childhood. Consequently, the discovery and articulation of it become equivalent to a *confession* of wrongdoing—a necessary step toward recovery. Medicine can then do its work. Thus, confession adds considerable psychological force to the disease sanction. In order to get well myself or perhaps to save the life of a child, I must suffer the shame of exposure involved in confession—although this may relieve my anxiety.

Confession is also the means by which knowledge of concrete cases of bad conduct become known along with the fact that they have been penalized by sickness. Among the Ojibwa, there is no isolation of a patient; the dwelling of a sick person is always full of people. Any statement made to the doctor soon becomes public knowledge. To confess a transgression is, in effect, to publicly reveal what may be a secret "sin." To the Ojibwa, however, this exposure is important. The very secrecy of misconduct is bad in itself, as for example, the violation of incest taboos. It is through confession in cases of illness that these become known. I obtained concrete examples of these by interviews with a contemporary medicine man who told me about cases of illness that he and his father had treated.

Sexual behavior is one of the major seedbeds of bad conduct that is believed to be penalized by sickness. The disease sanction reinforces the choice of approved sexual or marital partners, in accordance with the basic kinship structure already described. This mating and marital limitation narrows down to the choice of partners within the same kinship generation who call each other *ninam*. Sexually approved behavior is defined in terms of the position that individuals occupy in the social structure. All other matings are taboo.

At the same time, the disease sanction does not eliminate all sexually deviant conduct. Thus, when confession occurs, it reminds everyone in the community of the consequences of any departure from the choice of a sexual partner who is not addressed as *ninam*. Simultaneously, good sexual conduct is accentuated. Dynamically viewed, a society can tolerate a few breaches of the mores if a knowledge of such cases is a constant reminder to all to live a moral life and thereby avoid illness and possibly death. The only real danger to the social order would stem from an accumulative trend of actual conduct in a deviant direction, or from a direct challenge to primary values.

Another area of bad conduct in the interpersonal relations of human beings includes cruelty, murder, and overtly hostile or threatening acts such as verbal insults or gestures. All of these may be punished by illness. The disease sanction functioned to mute overt hostile acts in everyday life by making individuals feel guilty about them. Children were, in fact, warned against the display of aggressive behavior.

What about witchcraft? My guess would be that among the Ojibwa the number of persons believed to have met death by witchcraft far exceeded cases of actual homicide. And there is an interesting twist to Ojibwa thinking here as well. There can be no direct evidence, of course, that any act of witchcraft was performed. There can only be an *inference* on the part of the reputed victim or his friends, that he was the object of such a hostile act. The twist in thinking occurs because usually the reputed victim of witchcraft believes that by some act of his own he has *provoked* the witchcraft. It is he himself who has initiated the wrongdoing and thus provoked the penalty. The inner psychological pressure towards sharing, for example, is so strong that in one case, William Berens [1940] believed himself bewitched because he had overlooked one man. It was this man, he thought, who was responsible for giving him the "Indian disease," that is, projecting a material object into his body. In other words, the witchcraft in this case was a direct projection of the guilt he felt in not sharing.

Since no one wishes to be labeled a witch, confessions of witchcraft are rare. In all the case material on witchcraft that came to my attention, there was only one instance in which an old man, mortally ill, confessed to murder by witchcraft. It is interesting to note how this man rationalized his behavior. He confessed that he had killed two people a year for half a century! He said he was commanded to do this by his guardian spirits; otherwise he would have lost his own life. Since there is no appeal from the commands of "our grandfathers," the old man had an excellent defense. However, his confession did not prolong his life. He died, so that this case, too, could be interpreted as a punishment for bad conduct, however delayed.

What the disease sanction actually does in cases of aggression is to induce feelings of guilt in persons who become sick after they have overtly expressed some kind of hostile impulses in face-to-face relationships. The main function of the sanction then is not to penalize witchcraft or physical violence, but rather to motivate amiable social relations by reinforcing the suppression of aggressive impulses. The outwardly mild and placid traits of character the Ojibwa exhibit and the patience and self-restraint they exercise in personal relations are a culturally constituted facade that often masks hostile feelings. Individuals may wish to harm others, but fear retaliation through witchcraft should they expose their hostile impulses.

SELF-RELIANCE AND MORAL RESPONSIBILITY

There is an intimate connection then in the sociocultural system of the Ojibwa between the psychological reinforcement of self-discipline, the moral responsibility for conduct, and the stark realities inherent in their hunting and fishing economy. The integration of all these factors is to be seen in the characterological traits of the Ojibwa. Self-discipline underlies the self-reliance that is required of the hunter. It helps to build up ego strength, that is, the ability to cope realistically with the problem of making a living. Yet the achievement of this ego strength requires, at the same time, intimate social relations with and dependence upon other than human persons as well as human beings. It is here that the Ojibwa religious orientation and social order become integrated.

What was required was full moral responsibility for one's own conduct through meeting obligations to others. Hence, the obligations to other than human persons acquired in dreams could never be abrogated; they had to be fulfilled in some kind of future action. This relation between dreams and conduct gives the structure of the sociocultural system its distinctive stamp. The actors in the system, through appropriate socialization processes and institutions, were given a cognitive orientation to the universe and themselves that required participation in a wider than human society in order to fulfil their personal needs. Since obligations to other human persons were so highly individualized, personal, and secret, their fulfillment reinforced self-reliance, particularly since they were under an implacable disease sanction. At the same time, this severe penalty emphatically underlined in principle the importance of the fulfillment of obligations and reciprocal relations in *all* interpersonal conduct. Herein lay the moral unity in the entire Ojibwa world.

However self-reliant a man might strive to be, the vicissitudes of hunting compelled him to share the product of the chase with others, just as other than human persons shared their power with him. This, in turn, demanded amicable relations with other human beings and the suppression of any display of hostile impulses. Good conduct led to *pimädaziwin*—the Good Life—a feeling of security and confidence in facing the hazards of existence by being able to cope with all eventualities. Good dreams helped to promote this feeling as did good social relations. All this promoted ego strength, part of the price of which was self-control through self-discipline. Consequently, it was no accident when I discovered that group Rorschach data indicated the *least* acculturated Ojibwa to be better adjusted in terms of an optimum standard of mental health than the more highly acculturated groups where world view, values, and institutions were undergoing radical changes.[4]

PERSONALITY IN CULTURE

It is to be expected, then, that the Ojibwa type of personality functions through inner controls rather than outward coercion. What we find highly developed in individuals is a deep sensitivity to guilt and readiness to accept blame for conduct not socially sanctioned, which accounts for their hypochondriacal tendencies and the operation of a disease sanction as a major means of social control. In other words, social control operates through a psychological mechanism—the superego—in which self-punishment becomes prominent. This type of personality is a necessary correlate of a sociocultural system in which, for adults, there are no superordinate modes of social control.

Integrated with it is a world view in which the relations with other than human beings in dreams are related to conduct. Thus, the traditional interpretation of dreams may be considered a necessary factor in the operation of the sociocultural system of the Ojibwa. On the one hand, the meaning of dream experiences leads directly to the heart of the cognitive orientation towards the world with which their culture has provided them, and consequently towards their religion. The interpretation of dreams was based on their basic metaphysics of being—their conception of persons. In dreams it was possible for individuals to come into direct contact with the most powerful entities of the outer world of "reality" as defined in Ojibwa terms. On the other hand, these dreams had consequences that were related to the formation of the characterological traits of the actors in the system—the acquisition of specialized rules, decision making, and other forms of behavior. Dreaming assumed importance because of its effects upon behavior. Dreams linked the conceptual world of beliefs with conduct and with the values and choices that permeated the social order. What I have tried to indicate are the complex relations that existed between Ojibwa concepts, values, attitudes, institutions, individual experience, and the motivation of behavior in an ongoing sociocultural system.

Adaptation to "reality" in human evolution can never be understood as adaptation to a "reality" abstracted and projected from the physical and biological sciences as we now know them. Human survival has never been dependent upon the prior discovery of absolute truth or on a comprehensive objective understanding of all aspects of the world in which man found himself. The realities of human adaptation have always involved adaptation to the actualities of the world as meaningfully conceived, interpreted, and socially transmitted in cultural terms. Thus, ecological relations, historical processes, and the psychodynamics of individual adjustment must be considered with reference to cultural variables as an intermediary term. It is this cultural factor, along with man's capacity for self-awareness, that creates the human behavioral environment that is associated with the operation of every sociocultural system.

The Ojibwa are an example of how a people living in a harsh physical environment and equipped with a simple technology not only met the ecological and sociological requirements for survival, but created a viable world of their own conceptualization. This world had pragmatic value for them; it was a world in which they could think, dream, feel, and act. It survived until they began to be slowly drawn into another cultural world through their contact with the strange white man. But long after becoming ostensibly acculturated, small, relatively isolated groups retained living remnants of their old way of life and their traditional world view. It is from the remaining fragments of this world view that I have reconstructed as much of the whole as seems justified by the evidence.

EDITOR'S NOTES

1. A fuller text and analysis of this dream were published in Hallowell 1942:60–61. The conjurer's son was a "humpy" (humpback). As Berens remembered, "We boys were playing ball one day and I got [him] mad. I guess it was my fault. . . . [He] looked so funny when he ran that I ran the same way to tease him. All the boys laughed but he got mad and said to me, 'You'll remember this.' "

2. This phrasing is stronger than Hallowell's overall analysis suggests, and if queried, he might have modified it. The Ojibwa concern with illness and curing would not appear to connote the depression and imagined physical ailments of hypochondriacs as defined in dictionaries.

3. Several studies document extensive knowledge and curative use of plants among Ojibwa, Cree, and other groups. (See Densmore 1928, Leighton 1985, and Erichsen-Brown 1979, for example.) Hallowell did not examine the subject in great depth; the facts that much plant knowledge would be either privileged information revealed to individual men by their pawáganak, or else usually held by women (with whom Hallowell could not consult freely), restricted his access to the topic. Anna Leighton in her 1985 study recorded 78 plants used as herbal medicines by Woods Cree in Saskatchewan; and Charlotte Erichsen-Brown, in the introduction to her massive compilation, points out that the efficacy of many pre-20th-century European medical remedies was comparable to or less than that of many in the native North American pharmacopoeia.

4. The Rorschach test (developed by Hermann Rorschach, a Swiss psychiatrist) involves showing a series of inkblot designs to subjects whose responses give clues to their intellectual and emotional characteristics. Hallowell used the test in his Berens River fieldwork in 1938 and 1940, and then, with others, did comparative testing of the Lac du Flambeau Ojibwa of Wisconsin (1955:Chapter 5). The

results suggested to him that a range of Ojibwa personality types could be identified along an accultur-ational gradient, from the controlled, isolated, aboriginal type found in the inland Berens River communities to the increasingly less optimal levels of psychological adjustment found in personalities exposed to increased contact and the stress of change in Wisconsin. Some Berens River Ojibwa still remember Hallowell's showing those pictures; and as he himself recognized, the setting up of the testing situation across cultural boundaries, as well as the cross-cultural interpretation of results, presented great difficulties and challenges.

Appendix / Dwellings and Households along the Berens River [1935–36]

This section reviews the characteristic types of Berens River dwellings, giving special attention to aboriginal and adopted forms, to the changes that have occurred in the dwellings of the different settlements in the past 60 years [ca. 1870–1930], and to seasonal variations in housing.[1]

HOUSING: ADOPTED FORMS

Passing reference has been made to the log houses found today [1930s] in all of the settlements. These, of course, are not aboriginal types of dwellings. The generic form of such habitations (called *wakaiigan,* "house") was undoubtedly acquired by the Indians through their contacts with the fur traders, who usually constructed substantial buildings with gabled roofs, made of black or white spruce logs. Although some Berens River Indians, especially those associated with the Hudson's Bay Company, have copied these architectural features in the construction of their own dwellings, the ordinary log cabin of the Indian is a much simpler affair (Fig. 18). It is built of hewn jack pine logs, is flat-roofed (*napagígamik,* "flat [roof] house"), and seldom contains more than two or three rooms. Moss and dirt are spread upon poles laid across the rafters, and the wall logs are chinked with moss or mud—mud being preferable if it does not crack. The chief of the Pikangikum band, however, had a gable-roofed house under construction at Duck Lake when I was there in 1932. He proposed to shingle it with spruce bark.

Today [ca. 1935] the log cabin is the most common form of dwelling seen on the river. It has become the characteristic winter habitation in the upstream bands, and most of the Indians at the mouth occupy such houses year round. I was told, however, that the first log house built on the river by an Indian dated only from about 1873. It was erected by Cauwanäs on the site now occupied by the "H" on Map 3 of the Berens River Reserve. Ten years later, 33 log houses were reported at the mouth of the river (Dept. of Indian Affairs 1883:138). At that time the Indians up the river had not yet adopted this new type of dwelling; in 1888, when Chief Berens accompanied A. W. Ponton and his party up the river to survey the land

Figure 18. Tent and log house at Little Grand Rapids. The squared drum site in the foreground probably relates to the Drum Dance that Kiwitc received as a dream gift (see description in Hallowell 1955:160–163).

allotted to the Pikangikum Indians as a reserve (Bureau of Mines 1912:30), only one family at Little Grand Rapids was living in a log cabin. All the other families there and farther up the river were living in native dwellings. According to J. Moar, factor at the Little Grand Rapids post for 48 years, it was not until about 1914 that the Indians in this neighborhood seriously began to construct log cabins for themselves. Today, however, in addition to such structures built on the reserve and at Pauingassi for winter use, many of the Indians of this band, like those of the Pikangikum settlements, also have log houses built at some convenient wintering point on their hunting grounds. Roughly then, a period of only 20 years has elapsed since all the Indians of the Berens River except those at the mouth were housed in exclusively aboriginal fashion.

A less important nonaboriginal form of dwelling is the custom-made canvas tent (*pagwanígamik*), purchased from the traders. It is used sporadically in almost every settlement as a summer habitation. Many families of the Berens River band move into tents for the summer months. Some of them merely camp in their own "front yards" as it were, whereas others use tents while working for the commercial fishermen, often at some distance from their log dwellings.

The tent has long been used by the employees of the Hudson's Bay Company and probably has been in occasional use by the Indians at the mouth of the river almost as long as the log cabin. Compared with other dwellings, very few tents are to be seen up the river. But the Indians there often use canvas as a covering for their summer habitations.

ABORIGINAL DWELLINGS

Turning now to aboriginal dwellings, it is noteworthy that with perhaps one important exception, all of the various forms known in the past are still used today as occasion demands. The recently adopted forms described above simply have been added to the repertoire of native dwellings without completely supplanting them. One winter type of aboriginal dwelling is even to be found on the hunting grounds of some of the Indians from the mouth of the river, although, like the native summer dwellings, it has been completely replaced by adopted forms in the permanent settlement of the Berens River band.

There are three types of conically formed dwellings. The simplest in structure is the "brush tent" *(cingúbigan)*,[2] which is erected for temporary use only when traveling or hunting in winter. Trimmed poles are arranged in teepee formation and covered with the branches of spruce or balsam, tips downward. Additional poles are laid over the "brush" to keep it in place.

The second type is the bark-covered teepee *(pí'kogan)* (Fig. 19). The poles are of black spruce. When a camp is abandoned they are left standing, and new ones are cut at the next camping place. A three-pole foundation usually forms the structural nucleus of the dwelling, short crotches being left on the poles, which are interlocked at the top to give stability. Birchbark is still the typical covering when this form of habitation is in use, although canvas is sometimes employed to supplement the bark. The women prepare six or eight sheets of bark, about 12 to 19 inches in width and as long as can be obtained—the number of sheets necessary depends on the length. The women then carefully sew these sheets together with spruce roots, end to end, and bind them at the narrow ends with strips of white spruce. These teepee covers *(wigwásapakwe,* "birchbark cover") are rolled up when not in use, and can be easily carried from place to place or stored away. About 10 of them are necessary to cover a dwelling. When placed in position, they are shingled, and additional poles may be placed over them to help keep the bark in position. The inner side of the bark serves as the outer side of the dwelling. Cattail mats were formerly used to cover the lower part of a *pí'kogan,* to the height of some four feet from the ground. The bark would then be confined to the upper part of the structure. Skin coverings were never used for these dwellings or any of the others to be described. Formerly the *pí'kogan* was a type of dwelling in use during the entire year. At present, where used at all, it is only a summer habitation.

At the mouth of the river no conical dwellings of this sort are to be seen, nor have they been used there for 40 years or more. At Little Grand Rapids I have seen a few, and at Lake Pikangikum, out of a total of 19 summer dwellings, seven were of this type in 1932. There was one at Poplar Hill, but none at Duck Lake.

The third type of conical structure is called *mi'ti'gókiwam,* "wooden dwelling" (in colloquial English, "wooden tent"). An excellent example of this dwelling was seen at Lake Pikangikum; in the same settlement, another one, which had almost fallen apart, exhibited the same structural features. In the summer of 1934, a wooden tent in the Little Grand Rapids settlement was being used as a dog kennel for a litter of puppies. During the winter, however, it was inhabited by an old man and his wife. All these structures were about 10 feet in height, and 12–14

Figure 19. Pí'kogan *at Little Grand Rapids.*

feet in diameter. As in the *pí'kogan,* the fire was built in the center. Six unbarked spruce poles were used as a foundation. They were arranged in a fashion similar to the other conical dwellings. The "filling" is of 3–6-inch split jack pine poles. At the back of the dwelling these run upright, between the foundation poles, for the full length of the structure. On the sides they run obliquely to the foundation poles and are graduated in length.

The wooden framework is covered with moss *(äsakamik)* and earth, and the one observed at Lake Pikangikum was chinked here and there with old rabbit-skin blankets. A canvas door, with a stick arranged to spread the fabric, is usually provided.

This type of dwelling is characteristically a winter habitation, and the one seen at Lake Pikangikum, like the one at Little Grand Rapids, was occupied by an old couple. Many of the Indians from all sections of the river still live in these wooden

Figure 20. Wáginogan *framework. For covered examples, see Figure* 7.

tents on their hunting grounds. A photograph of a similar dwelling (locality not stated) appears in Godsell (1932:55).

Structurally distinct from the conical type of habitation is the hemispherical dwelling, or *wáginogan* ("bent [poles] dwelling"). It is constructed of a series of black spruce or willow poles planted vertically in the ground and bent over to form the roof. The poles are tied in place, and one or more horizontal poles are added to give stability to the structure (Fig. 20). The outer covering is of prepared birchbark rolls like those used for the *pí'kogan,* slabs of spruce bark (observed at the Pauingassi settlement, 1933), or canvas.

I was told that these are much easier to construct than a good *pí'kogan.* Willow poles are quite satisfactory for the *wáginogan* and much easier to obtain than the series of spruce poles of the proper length and size necessary for the *pí'kogan.* On the other hand, an open fire is not usually built in the *wáginogan,* as used on the Berens River. There is often, therefore, no source of heat or light in the dwelling. Besides, a stage for drying and smoking meat and fish must be erected outside the *wáginogan*—a feature taken care of in the *pí'kogan* itself. Nevertheless, at the present day, the *wáginogan* is the most widely used summer dwelling in the upriver settlements. It often contains a small iron stove with a short stretch of pipe leading directly upward through the roof.

Chief William Berens tells me that so far as he knows, this type of dwelling was never in use at the mouth of the river and that it is a relatively recent introduction inland, having been in vogue not more than 20 years! Yet it would appear to be an old and widespread type of habitation among the Algonquian peoples of the Eastern Woodlands,[3] and presumably in the region of the Great Lakes from which Ojibwa peoples migrated. It has even been considered one of the oldest forms of dwelling in North America. Personally I have no immediate answer to this historical paradox; nor do I see any reason to doubt Chief Berens.[4] The other native house types were quite adequate, and the association of the hemispherical dwelling with modern stoves may indeed be significant in this case. Furthermore, the recent use of this type of structure as a dwelling is in no way inconsistent with the knowledge and use of similar structures for other purposes. That such was the case is evidenced by the plan of construction followed in building ceremonial structures: the sudatory, or sweat lodge; the *wáginogan* (note the identity of the terms) used in conjunction with the midewiwin; the *midewígamik*[5]; and the present-day *wabanowígamik*. In form at least, if not in function, it appears probable that all of these structures antedated the hemispherical dwelling among the Berens River Indians, whatever may have been the case elsewhere. It seems more than likely, as Bushnell suggests (1919:612, 614), that the *wáginogan* was a more southerly form of habitation than either the conical birch-covered type of dwelling or the *cäbandawan,* the only remaining form of aboriginal habitation to be discussed.

A long triangular prism in shape, the *cäbandawan* was typically a multiple-family dwelling (Fig. 21). Against a ridgepole, supported at each end by four forked crossed poles, a series of light spruce poles was laid at an angle of 45 degrees to form the sides. The structure was then covered with birchbark,[6] or sometimes one row of cattail mats would be used, the rest of the covering being of bark. There was usually a fireplace in the center, and then one or more fires between this point and the door at either end of the dwelling, depending upon the number of families occupying it. The size of some of these structures in former times may be judged from a statement made to me at Island Lake (1930); Richard Munias told me that as a boy he had seen a *cäbandawan* at Sandy Lake with 10 fires. Usually two families, occupying opposite sides of the dwelling, made use of a single fire. In addition to the doors at each end, openings were left at each side, if more than four families occupied the dwelling. This was said to provide an easy exit and entrance for the women, who would not then have to pass through the center of the dwelling with the possibility of stepping over men's legs and belongings, which was strictly forbidden. Except for infants, the children were segregated according to sex. The girls slept on the side of the mother away from the father, and the boys on the side of the father away from the mother. This brought the men together in a group, and left the women to cluster around the doors.

The *cäbandawan* was always occupied by closely related persons—parents and their married children, married brothers, or a few generations back, by a man and his several wives (Cenawagwaskang and his six wives were repeatedly referred to as

Figure 21. Cäbandawan *on the lower Red River, Manitoba, in 1858. Photograph by Humphrey Lloyd Hime (compare woodcut in Hind 1860:202).*

an example of this type). The *cäbandawan* is the dwelling most frequently referred to in mythology, and the Berens River Ojibwa consider it to be the most characteristic type of the aboriginal period. This fact is worthy of consideration by those such as Birket-Smith and Waterman, who posit dwellings with a circular groundplan as being of greatest antiquity in North America.

The *cäbandawan* is the only aboriginal habitation that, in its typical form, has practically disappeared. In 1888, when Chief Berens visited Lake Pikangikum, the whole population was housed in either *cäbandawan* or *pi' kogan*. Indeed, all of the old men and women living up the river today, as well as most individuals over 25 years of age, spent either most of their lives or the early years of their childhood in these forms of habitation. Even in the summer of 1934, the Keepers, a large family of the Little Grand Rapids settlement, erected what was essentially a *cäbandawan*, although unlike the typical form, it had only a single door (Fig. 22).

Despite the fact that the *cäbandawan* has disappeared as a dwelling, characteristic dwelling clusters of closely related individuals who constitute subunits of the summer settlements may still be found although these individuals no longer sleep under a common roof. At a former period, when the *cäbandawan* was used as a year-round habitation, similar related groups shared these multiple-family dwellings. In the winter the log cabins now function as multiple-family dwellings in many instances, so that many of them become the modern equivalents, at this season, of the aboriginal *cäbandawan*. Consequently, I believe it is fair to state that although the physical aspects of housing have changed considerably during the

Figure 22. The Keeper family dwelling, Little Grand Rapids. This structure was the closest parallel to a cäbandawan *seen on the Berens River in the 1930s. Note the stovepipe and the mixture of bark and canvas coverings.*

recent period of acculturation, so far as the upstream bands are concerned, this change has not appreciably dislocated any of the social and economic patterns connected with the aboriginal manner of living.

HOUSEHOLD COMPOSITION

Some comments on the size and composition of household groups will elucidate the classification of dwelling types by outlining patterns of residency. It is worth noting in the first place that in not a single instance was an Indian found living alone. I venture to say that this would be an extremely rare occurrence. In this society, as a matter of fact, such a mode of life would be considered abnormal, especially in the case of women.

The relatively high proportion of dwellings that housed only two individuals, however, is somewhat striking. In more than half of these cases (16), a man and his wife were living alone. They were either couples past middle age, whose children had married, or they were childless or newly married. The remaining households were of miscellaneous composition, such as a widow and son, a young widower and child, a woman separated from her husband and living with her old father, two widowed sisters, two unmarried half-brothers (uterine, that is, having the same mother), and a middle-aged spinster and her bachelor brother (Berens River).

Although most of the dwellings housing three persons comprised a married couple and a child, two households of this class are worth a passing comment. One was a tent in the Poplar Narrows settlement in which three adolescent boys were living, next to the dwelling of their parents. The other instance was the *wáginogan* in the Duck Lake settlement occupied by three middle-aged spinster sisters. Both households were purely seasonal adjustments. During the winter these two summer household groups would disappear as separate entities.

Households containing four occupants were the mode when taken for the river as a whole, although not for each settlement. Practically all of them were single-family households, either simple or complex. A few are of special interest. In the Lake Pikangikum settlement, the dwelling occupied by the oldest couple of the band was also shared by their unmarried daughter (a middle-aged woman) and one of the old man's grandsons, a boy of 11, whose job was to help with all sorts of odd tasks. His parents lived in the same encampment. At Duck Lake two half-orphan children were being cared for by a childless old couple. The mother of the children was the daughter of the old man's brother, who also lives in the encampment and has assumed the care of two additional children of his deceased daughter. Another household that was somewhat aberrant comprised a woman and her three illegitimate children. In the winter she shared the dwelling of one of her brothers.

Single-family households ranged in size from two persons to as many as 11 persons. In fact, two of the three dwellings numbering 10 persons each were single-family households. This was also true of one of the two numbering 11 persons.

On the other hand, multiple-family households may contain only two couples. There were two instances of this at Little Grand Rapids. In one case a newly married daughter was living with her elderly parents, and a young married son and his wife were living in his father's dwelling. The dwelling that the former occupied was a large *wáginogan*. In the latter case the young people occupied a tent built into one side of a *wáginogan*.

The two households containing more than 11 persons, one at Duck Lake and the other at the mouth of the river, were the dwellings of the chief of the Pikangikum and Berens River bands, respectively. At Pikangikum, besides the chief's wife and five unmarried daughters, there lived under the same roof a widowed daughter and her three small children; and a married daughter, her husband, and their children. This last family occupied a canvas tent attached to the back of a large *wáginogan* in which the other 11 persons dwelt. This modern combination of a tent with a *wáginogan* as a means of accommodating a multiple-family group under one roof was observed in a number of other instances. This combination structure demonstrates that in certain cases, the aboriginal habits of communal living, torn from their old architectural matrix, have welded incongruous forms of dwellings into a mixed and novel form of habitable unit. The same process of readjustment is observable elsewhere. At Island Lake I recall one communal dwelling that consisted of a *pí'kogan* flanked on three sides by canvas tents.

At the mouth of the river, on the other hand, Chief Berens' household of 15 persons was accommodated in a modern form of two-story house, the only one of its kind on the reserve (Fig. 23). It was built for the manager of a fish hatchery no longer in operation. Besides his wife and several unmarried children, there lived in

Figure 23. The house occupied by Chief William Berens and his family at the mouth of the Berens River.

it two married sons, a widowed daughter and her children, and the son of his deceased brother.

The rarity of dwellings housing multiple-family groups, in contrast to the overwhelming preponderance of single-family households of the simple variety, is the most conspicuous pattern in the data. This pattern holds true for the households at the mouth of the river as well as for the inland settlements. But since the households at the mouth of the river are fairly stable in their size and composition throughout the year, just as those at the inland settlements are more distinctly variable, it appears that under the influence of modern conditions, the trend in household composition is definitely towards the single-family household. In composition, as in size, the contemporary population is tending towards a form of household antithetical to that of the aboriginal period.

This trend means that, as a rule, married individuals of distinct generations, except those with deceased spouses, no longer occupy the same dwelling. In the summer settlements up the river, only six married sons and five married daughters were members of the same household as their living parents, and at the mouth of the river such associations were even rarer. Widows, it may be added, were more frequently found in the households of their sons than of their daughters.

The modern trend has also displaced, at least in summertime, another household association pattern that was not uncommon in former days: the occupation of the same dwelling by married siblings, especially brothers, one or both of whose parents might be dead. In the data I collected, there was not a single case in which orphaned married brothers, married sisters, or a married brother and sister shared the same dwelling in summer. It is true that all three of these combinations occurred in winter in the upstream bands, but no such instances were found in the contemporary households of the Berens River band at the river mouth.

NOTES

1. [This section and notes 2–6 have been edited from A. I. Hallowell's unfinished manuscript, *Pigeon River People*, written in 1935–1936. It is included here because of its rich ethnohistorical detail and also because it dovetails so well (as Hallowell doubtless intended) with previously unpublished photographs of Berens River dwelling types. It also elucidates the discussions of settlement patterns in Chapter 4 and reminds us that "wigwam" and "teepee" are not Berens River Ojibwa categories; these words, from northeastern Algonquian and Siouan languages, respectively, have passed into English as generic terms for Indian dwellings.]

2. *Cingubik* is the generic term for the two varieties of spruce (black and white) and balsam; *-an* is the dependent suffix signifying a dwelling or shelter of some kind.

3. D. I. Bushnell, Jr. in "Ojibway Habitations and Other Structures" (1919:609) writes: "The habitations of the northern and central Algonquian tribes, from the coast westward to and including the greater part of the Ojibway, appear to have been quite similar. The dome-shaped wigwam predominated."

4. Contributory evidence from a settlemnt of Saulteaux farther north may be cited. When I visited Island Lake (1930), none of the Indians were living in dome-shaped structures, and my informants disclaimed knowledge of this form of dwelling.

5. Compare Bushnell (1919:615): "the Mide lodge, often a hundred feet or more in length, was in reality an elongated example of the *waginogan*. The frame was similarly constructed but often the covering was of a more temporary nature, boughs being occasionally used."

6. A woodcut entitled "Ojibway Tents on the Banks of the Red River, Near the Middle Settlement" (Hind 1860:202) gives a thoroughly accurate visual impression of one of these dwellings in the middle of the 19th century (compare Bushnell 1919:plate 2). Sometimes these structures were so long that a ridgepole made from a single tree was too short and another one was added. [See Fig. 21, this volume, for the photograph on which the Hind woodcut is based.]

Afterword

AN ETHNOGRAPHY OF EXPERIENCE

A. I. Hallowell would probably be sympathetic to some recent developments in anthropology and ethnographic writing. Analysts of current trends in interpretive anthropology seem not to cite his work, however. Possibly the text published here will lead some of them back to Hallowell as a harbinger of developments to which they sometimes assign a later date.

The past two decades have seen, as George Marcus and Michael Fisher tell us, a proliferation of "ethnographies of experience" that seek "novel ways to demonstrate what it means to be a Samoan, an Ilongot, or a Balinese, and in so doing, to persuade the reader that culture matters more than he might have thought." Marcus and Fisher perceive in these works a new focus on "conceptions of personhood—the grounds of human capabilities and actions, ideas about the self, and the expression of emotions," and credit Clifford Geertz in the early 1970s as helping to "initiate this move toward cultural definition of the person as an important focus of ethnography" (1986:43, 45, 47). Yet Hallowell was exploring that ground more than a decade earlier, notably in his 1960 article, "Ojibwa Ontology, Behavior, and World View" (reprinted in 1976a:Chapter 9), and his sensitivity to the importance of these domains deserves acknowledgment.

In some senses too, the ethnography published here was experimental for its time. Hallowell, with incomplete success, was trying "different textual strategies" and surely aspired, like his successors, "to write fuller and more richly evoked accounts of other cultural experiences" while also placing his subjects "firmly in the flow of historic events" (Marcus and Fisher 1986:43–44). His opening chapters historicize the Berens River Ojibwa more than his earlier writings, and implicitly he and William Berens together counter older views, persistent in some quarters, of native peoples as mythic, without their own historical constructs and consciousness (see Martin 1987:33, 195). In doing so, they also unfold the family history of Chief Berens and his ancestors as a kind of model for the ethnohistory of the whole of Berens River. Hallowell makes explicit his profound reliance on Berens, although without quite launching into the "confessional tale" genre of ethnography aptly described by Van Maanen (1988:Chapter 4) or the "heroic extremes of subjectivity" found in some recent work (cf. Brumble 1988:93). His second three chapters exhibit, amid all their cultural data, a strong focus on self and personhood, and hence also speak to current sensibilities.

In sum, this is not a classic comprehensive ethnography in the old style, covering all socioeconomic topics down to pots and pans; Hallowell (regrettably in some ways) abandoned such an enterprise when he set aside the writing of *Pigeon River People* in the late 1930s. Instead, this book, in its later chapters in particular, offers a selective weaving together of the themes and patterns of Ojibwa thought and character, which Hallowell ultimately found most significant, and perhaps appealing, after over three decades of thinking about his material. His continuing intellectual engagement with the Berens River Ojibwa, many years after his last visit to them, is nicely reflected both in these chapters and in a letter of 8 May 1961 summarizing his thoughts on "their culturally constituted life as hunters":

> On the one hand, they may be considered to have adapted themselves in part through highly positive knowledge of the fauna and flora of their physical environment. On the other hand they combine with this a cognitive orientation to a wider cosmos in terms of traditional beliefs and values (including myths) which are drenched with fantasy and imagination. Yet it is a successful life adjustment for individuals and adaptive for the group (Hallowell to David Beres, Hallowell Correspondence, APS).

HALLOWELL AND THE LIVING PAST

Of course, Hallowell's writings of the 1960s, like those of any complex thinker whose ideas evolve over time, also contain sedimentary deposits from all his prior decades of reading, research, and interaction with scholars of his own and prior generations. As a consequence, he at times typologizes the Ojibwa along cultural and social-evolutionary gradients that would have seemed less problematic to older audiences than they do now. Chapter 1, describing the voyage upriver to the "living past in the Canadian wilderness," describes the inland Ojibwa as being at "the aboriginal level of spatial orientation" and operating at "a more primitive level of temporal orientation." From an alternative perspective, however, we might ask whether people at his implied "modern" level do not in many situations resemble the Ojibwa in their own cognitive uses of landmarks and temporal markers, even when able to resort to maps and clocks.

   Similarly, Hallowell's conceptualization of an acculturational gradient along the Berens River presents a typology that raises several questions. First, there is a historical problem; the inland Ojibwa had had considerably more contact with the fur trade than Hallowell could have realized from the sources available to him, and hence were not as isolated historically as he supposed (Lytwyn 1986). Although they appeared traditional compared with the Ojibwa at the river's mouth, the complexity of the historical picture weakens the case for reading them as a kind of aboriginal baseline; indeed, trade contacts could have caused these Ojibwa to highlight certain adaptations and specialized activities that outsiders (or even they themselves) later read as "traditional." At the same time, as recent studies of the fur trade have indicated, Indian accommodations to the fur trade cannot simply be equated with dependency. (For further discussion and references see the review essay by Brown and Peers in Hickerson 1988.)

SITUATING THE BERENS FAMILY

The river mouth or "lakeside" people also need a second look. Although Hallowell considered William Berens to be "highly acculturated," his data offer grounds for questioning that assessment. When, in 1940, Hallowell wrote down the old chief's account of his life from the 1860s to the early 1900s, he recorded several episodes that demonstrated Berens' persisting strong Ojibwa values, outlooks, and beliefs (Brown 1989:211, 214–216). Hallowell never published this text or an analysis of it (although this book quotes occasionally from it), and one wonders if he sensed a certain tension between his representations of Berens and the chief's own life story. One striking feature of the Berens family and the lakeside community generally is the extent to which they in fact assimilated newcomers, new economic opportunities, and social and political changes for their own purposes, and within a strongly persisting value system; indeed, William Berens surely welcomed and accepted Hallowell among his people for purposes of his own, both personal and culturally based.

The Berens reminiscences themselves may be read in different ways. The chief's account of his successes in commercial fishing, fur trading, and other activities could be seen as a picture of an Indian entering the white man's world and leaving his heritage behind him. But it could also be viewed as an example of a traditional native literary genre widespread among adult males, the "coup tale," recounting personal achievements and honors. In older times, warriors would recount their exploits and strikes against their enemies, as a means of impressing and attracting followers (Brumble 1988:23–30); the Berens narrative might be taken as a moderate recasting of that mode of discourse.

Alternative readings of data are possible in other instances. Hallowell recounts the election of Jacob Berens as chief in 1875 and his beating of a powerful "medicine man" rival for that position (Chapter 3). The night after, when Jacob Berens began to feel sick, he became convinced that the other man was trying to "get him," a view much in accord with Ojibwa theories of disease. William Berens told Hallowell that Jacob "believed that the Christian faith he had adopted helped him to recover from his illness"; and Hallowell, in turn, took this attitude as a sign that Jacob "was already sloughing off his aboriginal values" (1976a:432).

Another perspective is possible, however, as we may learn from other instances in which mission Christianity has been indigenized (e.g., Kan 1988:214–216). Jacob may have sought and cultivated Christianity very much within an Ojibwa framework of seeking help from and access to whatever new kinds of *pawáganak*, or helping spirits, could enhance the powers and abilities already available to him. Unlike Christians, Ojibwas were not exclusionary in their view of religion, and the resources of Jacob Berens' Methodism were probably viewed as a potentially valuable adjunct to other sources of spiritual power. Acculturation theory has made bows towards asking how each party in a culture-contact situation modified or acculturated the other, and Hallowell himself explored such issues with much subtlety in some of his late writings (for example, 1976a:Chapters 12, 13). But in studying the Berens River Ojibwa, he sometimes assumed a one-way progression involving cultural loss and replacement, rather than a more complex complementarity or fusion.

"TACKLING THE WOMEN"

Reading Hallowell from a late 20th-century perspective, some may notice a relative lack of attention to women and gender. Yet Hallowell was never able to explore to his own satisfaction the roles and viewpoints of the women of Berens River; nor could he pursue any in-depth analysis of Ojibwa gender relations, given the social segmentation between male and female. In the summer of 1934, he brought to Berens River a graduate student, Dorothy Spencer, who would, he intended, "tackle the women." But, as he later explained in a letter to R. W. Dunning (27 October, 1955), they had interpreter trouble; the woman whom Spencer was to work with had moved away, and no satisfactory substitute could be found. Spencer was able to record a few myths but never continued in that field; her later research centered on Fiji and India.

If women and gender relations were not specific foci of Hallowell's publications, they nonetheless appeared frequently as subtexts in his writings and field notes, and it is possible to learn a considerable amount from him on these subjects. The chapters published here comment at several points on the economic roles of women as processors of food, firewood, birchbark, skins, and furs, as well as on their familial and kinship roles. In Hallowell's fieldwork of the 1930s, women emerged as having critical technical or technological skills, which they learned (it appears) in a rather secular, practical way from mothers and grandmothers. In this they contrasted with men for whom religious power and the dream quest for assistance from the *pawáganak* were central preoccupations if a man was to succeed in hunting, conjuring, curing, or simply attaining *pimädaziwin,* the Good Life. Women might dream and acquire spiritual power, but they did not have to do so.

This contrast in gender roles raises intriguing questions, given the concerns of many scholars with the pervasiveness of patriarchy in human history and, on the other hand, with current quests for egalitarian, communal societies where women's socioeconomic status might be declared equivalent (if not identical) to men's. If women were largely excluded from empowering dreams and the roles, skills, and opportunities that they conferred, and if (as Hallowell and others also found) they were subject to a wide range of menstrual and other taboos when it came to handling men's implements, eating certain bear parts, and so on, were they automatically the weaker victims, low in status, without recourse? Or was there a kind of power and status in not needing the *pawáganak* to achieve their skills and goals, and in the threats that they posed to males if they broke the taboos and conventions that protected the men from them?

It is possible that late 20th-century preoccupations with patriarchy and egalitarianism tell us more about ourselves than about the Ojibwa; at any rate, these matters offer food for endless and stimulating debate. One point does seem to emerge rather clearly, however. It seems useful, when looking at gender among the Ojibwa, and perhaps in all societies, to conceptualize male and female in cultural terms, as two subcultures that share and communicate on many levels but also maintain separateness, boundaries, and differences that never entirely disappear. This point has implications for our understandings of the Ojibwa (and countless other groups) as we try to comprehend them from the available sources. To what extent is our knowledge of Berens River Ojibwa culture, religion, and society gender-bound, mediated as it is through the close cooperation of two men, Berens and Hallowell, and their largely male informants?

Another speculative question concerns gender and language. In Chapter 5,

Hallowell (like other Algonquianists) noted that the Ojibwa language makes a formal grammatical distinction between animate and inanimate but not between genders. Human beings, most animals and plants, the sun, and the winds are animate; but most manufactured objects (utensils, clothing, canoes, dwellings, etc.), with pipes as a notable exception, are inanimate. As Hallowell observed, "animate" and "inanimate" are labels imposed from the outside. We might ask whether at some level gender actually remains a factor in this distinction, since manufactured products are so largely associated with women (pipes, with their religious significance, being presumably in a special category).

The divergent roles of women and men also deserve further examination under conditions of social change or (in Hallowell's framework) acculturation. Some recent studies have reached at least tentative conclusions that in some northern native communities, women, because of the dynamics of their past roles and occupations, have adapted better than their male counterparts to externally induced changes, pressures, and opportunities (Cruikshank 1983:25–26; Spindler and Spindler 1990; 1991). Hallowell's writings, both published and unpublished, may usefully be mined further for data bearing on all these questions, as may Ojibwa experiences and memories themselves, across recent centuries.

ETHNOGRAPHY AS HISTORY

This book, with its layers from the 1930s, the 1960s, and the 1990s, and with its Ojibwa, anthropological, and editorial voices, comes to an end; yet it should not be regarded as either closed or definitive. One quality shared by both the Ojibwa and Hallowell is that they open our minds to questions and issues that remain fresh and challenging, and to human histories and experiences that are endlessly rich and complex. "Pete" Hallowell and "Willie" Berens (as they were known to their respective friends) may still in some senses converse with us, as they once did at such length with each other. The ethnographic notes and papers and the individuals from whom they came are now a part of history. But they still have much to teach.

Jennifer S. H. Brown

References

Bellan, Ruben
  1978   *Winnipeg First Century: An Economic History*. Winnipeg: Queenston House Publishing.

Berens, William
  1940   Reminiscences. Transcript of oral narrative set down by A. Irving Hallowell. Hallowell papers, MS Coll. 26, American Philosophical Society, Philadelphia.

Bishop, Charles A., and Toby Morantz, eds.
  1986   Who Owns the Beaver? Northern Algonquian Land Tenure Reconsidered. *Anthropologica* 28 (1–2). Special issue.

Brown, Jennifer S. H.
  1980   *Strangers in Blood: Fur Trade Company Families in Indian Country*. Vancouver: University of British Columbia Press.
  1987a   The Métis: Genesis and Rebirth. In *Native Peoples, Native Lands: Canadian Indians, Inuit, and Métis,* Bruce A. Cox, ed. Ottawa: Carleton University Press, pp. 136–147.
  1987b   A Cree Nurse in a Cradle of Methodism: Little Mary and the E. R. Youngs at Norway House and Berens River. In *First Days, Fighting Days: Women in Manitoba History,* Mary Kinnear, ed. Regina, Saskatchewan: Canadian Plains Research Center.
  1989   A Place in Your Mind for Them All: Chief William Berens. In *Being and Becoming Indian: Biographical Studies of North American Frontiers,* James A. Clifton, ed. Chicago: Dorsey, pp. 204–225.
  1991   From Sorel to Lake Winnipeg: George Nelson as an Ethnohistorical Source. In *New Horizons in Ethnohistory: Papers of the Second Laurier Conference on Ethnohistory and Ethnology,* Huron College, University of Western Ontario, 1983, Barry M. Gough and Laird Christie, eds. Ottawa: Canadian Museum of Civilization, *Mercury Series*.

——— and Robert Brightman
  1988   *"The Orders of the Dreamed": George Nelson on Cree and Northern Ojibwa Religion and Myth, 1823*. Winnipeg: University of Manitoba Press/St. Paul: Minnesota Historical Society Press.

Brumble, H. David III
  1988   *American Indian Autobiography*. Berkeley: University of California Press.

Bureau of Mines
  1912   *Report on the Country in the Vicinity of Red Lake and Part of the Basin of Berens River*. Vol. 21, part II. Toronto.

Bushnell, David I., Jr.
  1919   Ojibway Habitations and Other Structures. *Annual Report of the Board of Regents of the Smithsonian Institution, 1917*. Washington, D.C.: pp. 609–623.

Cruikshank, Julie
  1983   The Stolen Women: Female Journeys in Tagish and Tutchone. National Museum of Man *Mercury Series,* Canadian Ethnology Service Paper no. 87. Ottawa.

Densmore, Frances
  1928   Uses of Plants by the Chippewa Indians. Bureau of American Ethnology, *Forty-fourth Annual Report*. Washington, D.C.: pp. 275–397.

Department of Indian Affairs
  1883   Report. Canada, *Sessional Papers*. Ottawa.

Dickason, Olive P.
  1989   Concepts of Sovereignty at the Time of First Contacts. In *The Law of Nations and the New World*, L. C. Green and Olive P. Dickason. Edmonton: University of Alberta Press, pp. 141–295.

Duckworth, Harry W.
  1988   The Madness of Donald Mackay. *The Beaver* 68(3):25–42.

Dunning, R. W.
  1959   *Social and Economic Change among the Northern Ojibwa*. Toronto: University of Toronto Press.

Erichsen-Brown, Charlotte
  1979   *Use of Plants for the Past 500 Years*. Aurora, Ont.: Breezy Creeks Press.

Fewkes, Vladimir J.
  1937   Aboriginal Potsherds from Red River, Manitoba. *American Antiquity* 3:143–155.

Francis, Daniel, and Toby Morantz
  1983   *Partners in Furs: A History of the Fur Trade in Eastern James Bay, 1600–1870*. Montreal: McGill-Queen's University Press.

Godsell, Philip H.
  1932   The Ojibway Indian. *Canadian Geographical Journal* 4(1):51–66.

Gottesman, Dan
  1988   Native People, Demography. *Canadian Encyclopedia*, 2nd ed., vol. 3. Edmonton: Hurtig, pp. 1448–1449.

Hallowell, A. Irving
  1926   Bear Ceremonialism in the Northern Hemisphere. *American Anthropologist* 27:1–175.
  1928   Was Cross-Cousin Marriage Practiced by the North-Central Algonkian? *Proceedings, Twenty-Third International Congress of Americanists* (New York), 519–544.
  1935–1936   *Pigeon River People*. Unpublished uncompleted manuscript. Philadelphia: American Philosophical Society.
  1938   The Incidence, Character, and Decline of Polygyny among the Lake Winnipeg Cree and Saulteaux. *American Anthropologist* 40:235–256.
  1939   Some European Folktales of the Berens River Saulteaux. *Journal of American Folklore* 52:155–179.
  1942   The Role of Conjuring in Saulteaux Society. *Publications of the Philadelphia Anthropological Society*, vol. 2. Philadelphia: Philadelphia Anthropological Society.
  1949   The Size of Algonkian Hunting Territories: A Function of Ecological Adjustment. *American Anthropologist* 51(1):35–45.
  1955   *Culture and Experience*. Philadelphia: University of Pennsylvania Press. (Reprinted 1988 by Waveland Press.)
  1976a   *Contributions to Anthropology: Selected Papers of A. Irving Hallowell*. Chicago: University of Chicago Press.

1976b [1937]   Cross-Cousin Marriage in the Lake Winnipeg Area. In *Contributions to Anthropology: Selected Papers of A. Irving Hallowell*. Chicago: University of Chicago Press.

n.d.   Rocks and Stones. Unpublished typescript, 8 pp. Philadelphia: American Philosophical Society.

Harris, R. Cole, and Geoffrey J. Matthews
1987   *Historical Atlas of Canada*, vol. 1, *From the Beginning to 1800*. Toronto: University of Toronto Press.

Hawthorne, H. B.
1966   *A Survey of the Contemporary Indians of Canada: Economic, Political, Educational Needs and Policies*. Part 1. Ottawa: Indian Affairs Branch.
1967   Ibid, Part 2.

Helm, June, ed.
1981   *Subarctic. Handbook of North American Indians*, vol. 6. Washington, D.C.: Smithsonian Institution.

Henry, Alexander [the Elder]
1969   *Travels and Adventures in Canada and the Indian Territories between the Years 1760 and 1776*. James Bain, ed. (First edition 1809).

Hickerson, Harold
1962   The Southwestern Chippewa: An Ethnohistorical Study. *American Anthropological Association Memoir* 92, vol. 64(3), part 2.
1988   *The Chippewa and Their Neighbors: A Study in Ethnohistory* (revised and expanded edition prepared by Jennifer S. H. Brown & Laura L. Peers). Prospect Heights, IL: Waveland Press.

Hind, Henry Youle
1860   *Narrative of the Canadian Red River Exploring Expedition of 1857*. London. (Reprint 1971, Edmonton: Hurtig.)

Howard, James H.
1977   *The Plains-Ojibwa or Bungi*. Lincoln, Nebraska: J and L Reprint Company.

Kan, Sergei
1985   Russian Orthodox Brotherhoods among the Tlingit: Missionary Goals and Native Response. *Ethnohistory* 32(3):196–223.

Kane, Paul
1968 [1859]   *Wanderings of an Artist among the Indians of North America from Canada to Vancouver's Island and Oregon through the Hudson's Bay Company's Territory and Back Again*. Edmonton: Hurtig.

Kohl, Johann Georg
1985   *Kitchi-gami: Life among the Lake Superior Ojibway*. St. Paul: Minnesota Historical Society Press (1st ed. 1860).

Kroeber, Alfred L.
1934   Native American Population. *American Anthropologist* 36:1–25.
1939   Cultural and Natural Areas of Native North America. *University of California Publications in American Archaeology and Ethnology* 38. Berkeley.

Leighton, Anna L.
1985   Wild Plant Use by the Woods Cree (Nihithawak) of East-Central Saskatchewan. Ottawa: National Museum of Man *Mercury Series. Canadian Ethnology Service Paper* No. 101.

Long, John S.
  1986   " 'Shaganash': Early Protestant Missionaries and the Adoption of Christianity by the Western James Bay Cree, 1840–1893." Ed.D. dissertation, University of Toronto.

Lytwyn, Victor P.
  1986   *The Fur Trade of the Little North: Indians, Pedlars, and Englishmen East of Lake Winnipeg, 1760–1821.* Winnipeg: Rupert's Land Research Centre, University of Winnipeg.

Marcus, George E., and Michael M. J. Fischer
  1986   *Anthropology as Cultural Critique: An Experimental Moment in the Human Sciences.* Chicago: University of Chicago Press.

Martin, Calvin, ed.
  1987   *The American Indian and the Problem of History.* New York and Oxford: Oxford University Press.

Masson, L. R., ed.
  1960   *Les Bourgeois de la compagnie du Nord-Ouest.* 2 vols. New York: Antiquarian Press (1st ed. 1889–1890).

McColl, Frances
  1989   *Ebenezer McColl, "Friend to the Indians."* Winnipeg: privately printed.

Meyer, David
  1987   Time Depth of the Western Woods Cree Occupation of Northern Ontario, Manitoba, and Saskatchewan. *Papers of the Eighteenth Algonquian Conference,* William Cowan, ed. Ottawa: Carleton University, pp. 187–200.

Morris, Alexander
  1880   *The Treaties of Canada with the Indians of Manitoba and the North-West Territories.* Toronto: Belfords, Clarke, and Co.

Peers, Laura L.
  1987   "An Ethnohistory of the Western Ojibwa, 1780–1830." Master's Thesis, University of Winnipeg.

Peterson, Jacqueline, and Jennifer S. H. Brown, eds.
  1985   *The New Peoples: Being and Becoming Métis in North America.* Winnipeg: University of Manitoba Press/Lincoln, NE: University of Nebraska Press.

Pettipas, Katherine
  1980   An Ethnohistory of The Pas Area, Prehistoric–1875: A Study in Cree Adaptation. *Directions in Manitoba Prehistory: Papers in Honour of Chris Vickers,* Leo Pettipas, ed. Winnipeg: Association of Manitoba Archaeologists, pp. 169–232.

Redfield, Robert
  1952   The Primitive World View. *Proceedings of the American Philosophical Society,* 96:30–36.

Ritzenthaler, Robert E.
  1953   Chippewa Preoccupation with Health: Change in Traditional Attitude Resulting from Modern Health Problems. *Bulletin of the Public Museum of the City of Milwaukee* 19(4):175–257.

Rogers, Edward S.
  1962   The Round Lake Ojibwa. Art and Archaeology Division, *Occasional Paper* 5. Toronto: Royal Ontario Museum.

1978   Southeastern Ojibwa. *Handbook of North American Indians,* vol. 15, *Northeast,* 760–771, Bruce G. Trigger, ed. Washington, D.C.: Smithsonian Institution.

1981   History of Ethnological Research in the Subarctic Shield and Mackenzie Borderlands. *Handbook of North American Indians,* vol. 6, *Subarctic,* June Helm, ed., pp. 19–29. Washington, D.C.: Smithsonian Institution.

———— and Mary Black Rogers

1978   Method for Reconstructing Patterns of Change: Surname Adoption by the Weagamow Ojibwa, 1870–1950. *Ethnohistory* 25(4):319–345.

1982   Who Were the Cranes? Groups and Group Identity Names in Northern Ontario. *Approaches to Algonquian Archaeology,* Margaret G. Hanna and Brian Kooyman, eds. Calgary: University of Calgary Archaeological Association, pp. 147–188.

———— and J. Garth Taylor

1981   Northern Ojibwa. *Handbook of North American Indians,* vol. 6, *Subarctic,* June Helm, ed. Washington, D.C.: Smithsonian Institution, pp. 231–243.

Ross, Alexander

1972   *The Red River Settlement: Its Rise, Progress, and Present State.* Edmonton: Hurtig (1st ed. 1856).

Ryerson, John

1855   *Hudson's Bay: A Missionary Tour in the Territory of the Hon. Hudson's Bay Company.* Toronto: Missionary Society of the Wesleyan Methodist Church.

Salisbury, Richard

1986   *A Homeland for the Cree: Regional Development in James Bay, 1971–1981.* Montreal and Kingston: McGill-Queen's University Press.

Schoolcraft, Henry R., comp.

1839   *Algic Researches, Comprising Inquiries Respecting the Mental Characteristics of the North American Indians.* 2 vols. New York: Harper and Brothers.

Speck, Frank G.

1923   Mistassini Hunting Territories in the Labrador Peninsula. *American Anthropologist* 25(4):452–471.

1927   Family Hunting Territories of the Lake St. John Montagnais and Neighbouring Bands. *Anthropos* 22:387–403.

Spindler, George, and Louise Spindler

1990   Male and Female in Four Changing Cultures. *Personality and the Cultural Construction of Society: Papers in Honor of Melford E. Spiro,* David K. Jordan and Marc J. Swartz, eds. Tuscaloosa: University of Alabama Press, pp. 182–200.

1991   Rorschaching in North America in the Shadow of Hallowell. *The Psychoanalytic Study of Society,* Bruce Boyer, ed. Forthcoming.

Spiro, Melford E.

1976   Obituary of Alfred Irving Hallowell. *American Anthropologist* 78:608–611.

Steinbring, Jack H.

1980   An Introduction to Archaeology on the Winnipeg River. *Papers in Manitoba Archaeology* no. 9. Winnipeg: Department of Cultural Affairs and Historic Resources, Historic Resources Branch.

1981   Saulteaux of Lake Winnipeg. *Subarctic Handbook of North American Indians,* vol. 6. June Helm, ed. Washington, D.C.: Smithsonian Institution, pp. 244–255.

Syms, E. Leigh
1982   Identifying Prehistoric Western Algonquians: A Holistic Approach. *Approaches to Algonquian Archaeology: Proceedings of the Thirteenth Annual Conference,* Margaret G. Hanna and Brian Kooyman, eds. Calgary: Archaeology Association of the University of Calgary, pp. 1–34.

Tanner, Helen H., ed.
1987   *Atlas of Great Lakes Indian History.* Norman, OK: University of Oklahoma Press.

Thistle, Paul C.
1986   *Indian-European Trade Relations in the Lower Saskatchewan River Region to 1840.* Winnipeg: University of Manitoba Press.

Thwaites, Reuben G., ed.
1896–1901   *The Jesuit Relations and Allied Documents: Travel and Explorations of the Jesuit Missionaries in New France, 1610–1791.* 73 vols. Cleveland. (Reprinted: Pageant, New York, 1959.)

Townsend, Joan
1983   Firearms against Native Arms: A Study in Comparative Efficiencies with an Alaskan Example. *Arctic Anthropology* 20(2):1–33.

Van Kirk, Sylvia
1980   *"Many Tender Ties": Women in Fur-Trade Society, 1670–1870.* Winnipeg: Watson and Dwyer/Norman, OK: University of Oklahoma Press.

Van Maanen, John
1988   *Tales of the Field: On Writing Ethnography.* Chicago: University of Chicago Press.

Vecsey, Christopher
1983   *Traditional Ojibwa Religion and Its Historical Changes.* Philadelphia: American Philosophical Society, Memoir no. 152.

Wallace, Anthony F. C.
1980   Alfred Irving Hallowell. National Academy of Sciences, *Biographical Memoirs* 51:194–213.

Williams, Glyndwr, ed.
1975   *Hudson's Bay Miscellany 1670–1870.* Winnipeg: Hudson's Bay Record Society, vol. 30.

Young, Egerton R.
1890   *By Canoe and Dog-Train among the Cree and Saulteaux Indians.* Toronto.

Index

A

aboriginal-white contact, 24–25
acculturation, 8, 22, 36, 37–38, 112, 113.
    See also cultural change and continuity
    (among Ojibwa)
Algonquian peoples, 6
Amo (Victoria, wife of Bear), 24
animals
    giant, 61, 73
    prescribed treatment of, 62
    spirit owners of, 62–64, 68–69, 72, 82
animate/inanimate, concepts of, ix, 61, 115
anthropology, psychological, x, 111
archeology, 17
architecture. *See* dwellings; structures, cere-
    monial
Assiniboine (people), territory and location of,
    11, 20–21
avoidance, 56. *See also* taboos
    and gender, 54
    social functions of, 54–55
    of women, 88

B

bands, creation of, 35–36, 37, 49–50
Barner, Arthur, 29
baseline in ethnography, 112
Bear (Mahquah, c.1790–1871), 12, 13,
    14n.2, 15n.6
bear walkers (human persons in bear shape),
    67
Berens, Jacob (c.1829–1917), xii, 13, 29,
    38n.1
    Christian faith of, 113
    election as chief, 33, 34, 35, 113
Berens, Joseph, Jr., 6, 25
Berens, Mary McKay, 11, 13, 15n.3
Berens, William (c.1865–1947), xii, 3, 6, 10
    ill., 58 ill.
    cultural persistence in, 112–113
    dreams of, 85–87, 90
    family of, 7 ill.
    life history of, 13–14
Berens family
    history of, 11–14
    use of family names, 12–13, 15n.7, 25.
        See also Amo (Victoria), wife of Bear;
        Cauwanäs (Roderick Ross); Yellow Legs
        (c.1750–c.1830)
Berens River, 6, 8, 9 ill., 14n.2, 43
Bittern, Antoine, 10 ill.

blessings
    bestowed in dreams, 87
    and names, 12–13, 82
    reciprocal obligations of, 92
    role of gender in, 88
    secret nature of, 89
Boas, Franz, xiv
Boyer, Bryce, x
Boyer, Ruth, x
British North America Act, 1867; 30–31, 32
British Wesleyan Methodist Missionary Soci-
    ety, 28
brothers, 53
Brown, Jennifer S. H., vii, viii–ix
Bullhead lineage, 23 map, 24
Bungi, 21, 26n.5
burial customs, 74
Butikofer, Gary, recollections of Hallowell,
    xvii

C

cäbandawan. See dwellings, aboriginal
calendar, Ojibwa, 8, 43
Canadian Shield
    and aboriginal demography, 16
    description of, 16–17
cannibals. *See windigowak*
Caribou clan, 24
Case Studies in Cultural Anthropology, vii, xi
causation, Ojibwa concepts of, 71–72, 73,
    93
Cauwanäs (Roderick Ross), 12, 100
Cenawagwaskang, 24, 25
    marriages of, 24, 57, 105–106
Chatique (The Pelican), 26n.7
chiefs, 27n.9, 50
    creation of, 25, 35, 36
    political role of, 93
Chippewa, 6
Christianization. *See also* religion, Ojibwa
    acceptance and resistance to, 29, 113
    and decline of polygyny, 29–30
Churchill, Manitoba, 4
clan system (Ojibwa), 22, 26n.7. *See also*
    lineages
    as source of identity, 51
Confederation, effects of on Ojibwa, 30–31
confession, role of in healing, 94–95
conjuring, 4. *See also* shaking tent
    in Ojibwa religion, 82
    role of in healing, 68

cousins, 56, 57, 59n.4
creation of species, Ojibwa explanation of, 73
creation of the world, Ojibwa explanation of, 71, 72
Cree
   of Cross Lake, 4
   territory and location of, 11, 20–21
cultural change and continuity (among Ojibwa), 4, 5, 8, 10, 14, 17–21, 26, 36, 37–38, 45–46, 49–50, 112–113, 113. *See also* acculturation
   and Jacob Berens, 13, 113
   role of dreams in, 89–90
   role of language in, 60
   and William Berens, 112–113
cultural origins of Ojibwa, 17
culturally constituted world, concept of, ix, 14, 80
Culture and Experience, (Hallowell 1955), xii
customary use, 45

D

dances and dancing, 9, 10, 74
The Dead, 74–79
   burial position of, 74
   communication with, 75–78
   Feast of, 76
   food of, 75, 76
   Ghost dance, 77 ill.
   gifts to, 75–78
   Land of, 74
   reincarnation of, 78–79
   relations with, 76, 78
The Dead, Land of, 75
debt in fur trade, 17–18, 46
demography, aboriginal, 5, 6, 11, 16, 20–22, 24, 46, 48. *See also* population, aboriginal
"dependency" and Ojibwa, 18–20, 26, 112
directions, cardinal, 74
disease. *See also* health and healing; illness
   attitude towards, 93
   Ojibwa theory of, 113
diseases, infectious, in aboriginal times, 93
djibaiaking (Land of Ghosts). *See* The Dead, Land of
Dominion Lands Act, 1872, 31
dream visitors *(pawáganak). See* dreams and dreaming
dreams and dreaming, 84–92, 97–98
   and blessings, 87
   cultural persistence of, 89
   and dream visitors *(pawáganak),* 68, 87
   and fasting, 87–88
   and male prepuberty fast, 87
   and metamorphosis, 89
   and naming, 12–13, 59
   and out-of-body experience, 85, 87
   reality of, ix, 85

role of in sociocultural system, 86, 90
   of William Berens, 85–87, 90
   Yellow Leg's stone dream, 12
drums and drumming, 9, 10
   for The Dead, 77 ill., 77–78
Duck, John, 84 ill.
Duck lineage, 23 map, 24
dwellings, aboriginal, x
   arrangement of, 48–49
   cäbandawan (multiple family house), 49, 105–107
   cingúbigan (brush tent), 102
   mi'ti'gókiwam (wooden tent), 102–104
   pi'kogan (bark-covered teepee), 49, 102, 103 ill., 108
   wáginogan (bent poles), 104–105
dwellings, adopted forms
   log cabins, 10, 49, 100–101
   napagígamik (flat roofed house), 100
   pagwanígamik (canvas tent), 101
   wakaiigan (house), 100

E

environment
   behavioral, 63
   effect of on aboriginal life, 43, 46
   effect of on aboriginal population, 16
   and fur trade, 17
ethnic identity. *See* identity, group
ethnographic present, use of, xv, xvi, 112
ethnography
   ethics concerning informant identities, xvi
   historicizing of, xvi, 111
ethnohistory, xiii, xv, 26n.7
ethnonyms, 5–6, 15n.4, 21, 26n.5. *See also* identity, group
   for Ojibwa, 14n.1
Evans, James, 4, 28

F

Fair Wind (Nämawin, 1851?–1944), 25, 70, 83 ill.
   drum dance of, 77 ill., 78 ill.
fasting
   and dreams, 87–88
   and sexual purity, 88
Feast of the Dead. *See* The Dead, Feast of
feasting, 87–88
fishing settlements, summer, 44, 46–50, 47 ill.
flags, 75 ill.
The Flood in Ojibwa cosmology, 73
Fogelson, Raymond, xiii
food of the dead. *See* The Dead, food of
food taboos. *See* taboos
Frogs, Great, 61, 66, 73
fur trade
   and debt system, 17–18, 46
   effect of on Ojibwa, 17–20

G

gender
  and animate/inanimate concept, 115. *See also* language, Ojibwa, and gender
  and avoidance, 54
  lack of information about, 113–114
  and male prepuberty fast, 88
  and occupation, 9, 18, 44, 49, 88, 102, 113, 114
genealogies, Ojibwa, 11, 22, 51
ghosts. *See* The Dead
Ghosts, Land of. *See* The Dead, Land of
Gitchi Manitu (High God), 72
God, Ojibwa concept of, 72
Goldenweiser, Alexander, xiv
"Good Life," 82–85, 97
government, aboriginal, 36, 49–50
"grandfathers, our" (persons other than human). *See* "our grandfathers" (persons other than human)
grandparents
  and naming, 12–13
  social relations with, 57–59
  as storytellers, 65
graves, 74, 75, 76, 76 ill.

H

Hallowell, A. Irving, xvii, 10 ill.
  acculturation theory of, 112, 113
  career of, vii–viii, xiv–xv
  childhood and education of, xiii–xiv
  and Ojibwa fieldwork, xi
  typology in work of, 112
healers *(manāo)*, 12, 94
health and healing, 11–12, 93. *See also* illness; medicine, Ojibwa; Midewiwin (Grand Medicine Lodge)
  and confession, 94–95
  and conjuring, 68
  and dreams, 85–87
Henry, Alexander (The Elder), 20–21, 26n.7
household composition, 48–50, 107–109
  and kinship, 109
human and other than human persons. *See* persons, human and other-than-human
hunters and relations with animal "owners," 62–63
hunting groups, winter, 44
hunting territories, 44–46, 59n.2, 59n.3
hypochondria, 98n.2

I

identity, group, 26n.6. *See also* ethnonyms
  of Mary McKay Berens, 15n.3
  of William McKay, 15n.8
identity, personal, 50, 51. *See also* health and healing
  anthropological concepts of, 111
  and clan membership, 51
  concepts of, 50–51, 111

construction of, x
  and kinship terms, 50–51
  and names, 81
illness
  diagnosis in shaking tent, 68
  and hypochondria, 98n.2
  as penalty for wrong-doing, 92–93, 94
  as a result of rivalry, 113
  and sexual misconduct, 95
  and violent acts, 95
inanimate, concept of the. *See* animate/inanimate, concepts of
incest taboo. *See* taboos
inheritance of hunting territory, 45
Island Lake, 4–5

J

joking relationships, 55
justice system, Ojibwa, 93

K

kadabendijiget. *See* animals, spirit owners of
Kane, Paul, 5
S.S. *Keenora* (lake boat), 6, 7 ill., 10
Keeper, Joe, 10 ill.
Keeper family, 106
kinam. *See* "sweethearts"
Kingfisher lineages, 23 map, 24
kinship. *See also* avoidance; clan system; kinship terms
  and residence, 44, 48, 49, 51, 53, 105–107
  and social organization, 50–52
kinship terms, 50–57, 59n.4
  and generational distinctions, 52
  and in-laws, 52, 56
  for persons other than human, 65
  social functions of, 52–53

L

Lake Pikangikum people, 8–10, 47 map, 48
Lake Winnipeg, 17
Lake Winnipeg treaty. *See* Treaties, Treaty 5
land rights, extinguishment of aboriginal, 30, 32, 38
language, Ojibwa. *See also* kinship terms
  animate/inanimate concepts in, 61, 115
  and cultural persistence, 60
  gender in, 61, 72, 114–115
  and personal identity, 50
  and social organization, 50–51
languages, Algonquian, 6
life after death, 74–75
lineages, 23 map
literature, oral
  aboriginal style in, 113
  "truth" of, 81
Longfellow, Henry W., 5
Loon clan, 23 map, 24

M

Mahquah. *See* Bear (Mahquah, c.1790–1871)
manäo. See healers
Manitoba history and description, 11, 30–31
marriage, 51–52, 56–57. *See also* polygyny
  endogamous and exogamous, 51–52
  of human and other than human persons,
    66, 67
  and incest taboo, 54–55
  preferential, 57
  of "sweethearts," 56
material culture of Ojibwa. *See* Ojibwa, material culture
matrilocality, 44
McColl, Ebenezer, 31, 39f.2
McDougall, George, 29
McKay, William, 13, 15n.8
medicine, Ojibwa, 11–12, 83–84, 89. *See
  also* health and healing
  inefficacy of, 93
Medicine Lodge. *See Midewiwin*
medicine men
  political power of in aboriginal societies, 36
memengwéciwak (persons other than human)
  11, 12, 64. *See also* persons other than human in shaking tent, 70
  and medicine, 89
men
  occupations of, 9, 113
  and prepuberty fast, 88
  and special relations with spirit beings, 88
menopause and female occupations, 88
metamorphosis, 66–67, 73, 89
metaphysics, Ojibwa, 63, 81
Metis, 26n.6
  emergence of in Red River, 21
Midewiwin (Grand Medicine Lodge), 9, 11,
  12, 14, 36, 84. *See also* health and healing
Mikinak (The Great Turtle), 65, 67, 70
missions and missionaries. *See* Christianization; religion, Ojibwa
Moose clan, 22–23, 23 map
Moose lineage, 24
morality and moral order, 91–92, 96–97
Morris, Alexander, 35
Mosquitoes, Great, 73
myths and myth-telling, xvii, 65–66, 67. *See
  also* literature, oral
  about *cäbandawan,* 106
  about giant animals, 73
  appropriate season for, 65
  and concepts of time, 73
  as expression of worldview, 66

N

names and naming, 12–13, 58–59. *See also*
  Berens' family use of family names
  blessings of, 82
  of geographical features, 14n.2
  of Ojibwa clans, 24
  and personal identity, 81
    in reincarnation, 79
    role of dreams in, 59
    use of family names, 13, 25
names (group). *See* ethnonyms
nature and natural world in Ojibwa worldview, 81
ninam and *ninamak. See* "sweethearts"
nonsiblings, 53, 55
North West Company, 24–25
Northern Ojibwa, 14n.1, 22
Norway House, 4, 28

O

Oblate Fathers (Oblates of Mary Immaculate),
  29
occupational segregation. *See* gender and
  occupation
occupational units. *See* fishing settlements;
  hunting groups
occupations, 9, 44, 88. *See also* gender and
  occupation
  of men, 9, 113
  of women, 9, 18, 49, 88, 102, 114
Ohkanchiish, 19 ill.
Ojibwa
  cultural diversity of, 14n.1, 21
  cultural origins of, 17
  economic activities of before 1600, 17–20
  ethnonyms for, 5–6, 14n.1, 15n.4, 21,
    26n.5
  history of, 24
  material culture change after c.1700, 25–
    26
  material culture of before 1600, 17–18
  Northern, 14n.1, 22
  northern expansion of, 21–22
  Plains, 14n.1, 21, 22
  Saulteaux, 4, 5, 21
  social organization and language of, 50–52
  Southwestern, 21
  territory and location of, 6
  westward expansion of, 5–6, 20–22
"our grandfathers" (persons other than human), 59, 65. *See also* persons, human and
  other than human
  dream communication with, 84–85
  relations with, 67
  and sharing, 91
  and storytelling, 65
"our grandfather's" rock, 58 ill.
Owen, John. *See* Fair Wind (Nämawin,
  1851?–1944)

P

patrilineality, 13
  and kinship terms, 53
patrilocality, 44
pawáganak (dream visitors), 68, 87
Peguis (Ojibwa chief), 21
Pelican lineages, 23 map, 24, 26n.7
personality, Ojibwa, 96, 97–98, 98n.4

personhood. *See* identity, personal
persons
    concepts of, ix, x
    dual nature of human, 74–75
    human and other than human, ix
        relations of, 67–68, 70, 97
    and metamorphosis, 66–67
    power of human, 90–91
persons other than human, 10, 63–64
    communication with, 87
    and dreams, 59, 85
    human dependence on, 73–74, 80, 81, 82
    immortality and immutability of, 73–74
    relations with, 68–71, 88
    sex of, 65
    in shaking tent, 68–71
Pigeon River, 6
Pigeon River People (Hallowell ms.), x, xi,
    xii, xv, 27n.8, 111–112
pimädaziwin. See "Good Life"
Plains Ojibwa, 21, 22
plants
    prescribed treatment of, 62, 81
    spirit owners of, 62
    use of by women, 9, 98n.3
    use of in healing, 83, 93, 98n.3
political autonomy, aboriginal, 32
political power in aboriginal societies, 36
polygyny, 57. *See also* Cenawagwaskang,
    marriages of
    and Christianity, 29–30
Ponton, A. W., 100
Poplar River people
    in Treaty 5 territory, 36–37
population, aboriginal, 24, 39n.3. *See also*
    demography, aboriginal population, Ojibwa,
    39f.3
    of summer settlements in 1932, 48–49
    in Treaty 5 territory, 6, 33, 36, 37
power
    dreamed sources of, 84–85
    of human and other than human persons,
        81
    of human individuals, 90–91
    in shaking tent, 82
    sharing of, 87
    of women, 114
Proclamation of 1763, 32
property rights, 46

Q
Quill, Helen (Mrs. Stanley), 19 ill.

R
reality. *See* dreams and dreaming, reality of
reincarnation, 78–79
religion, Ojibwa, 81. *See also* Christianization
    Christian influence on, 28, 82, 113
religious behavior, 82–84
residence
    and kinship. *See* kinship and residence

Roe, Ann
    biographical interviews by, xvi
Rogers, Edward S., 3
Rorschach test, x, xiv, 97, 98n.4
Ross, Roderick. *See* Cauwanäs (Roderick
    Ross)
Rupert's Land, 3 map, 17
    transfer of to Canada in 1870, 30
Ryerson, John, 29

S
Saulteaux, 4, 5, 21. *See also* Ojibwa
Schoolcraft, Henry R., 5
schools on reserves, 33
Schultz, John Christian, 31
seasonal movements, 43–44, 46
sexual behavior. *See also* "sweethearts"
    as cause of illness, 95
sexual taboos. *See* taboos
shaking tent, 4, 10, 68–71, 69 ill.
    and out-of-body experience, 85
    as source of power and knowledge, 82
sharing, 46, 91–92. *See also* property right
siblings, 53, 54–55, 56
sisters, 53
smoke, ceremonial, 62, 74
Snakes, Big, 61, 63, 66, 73
sociocultural units, 43 44, 46
Song of Hiawatha (Longfellow), 5
Southwestern Ojibwa, 21
Speck, Frank, xiv, 59n.3
Spencer, Dorothy, 114
Spindler, George and Louise, xi, xvii
    and Hallowell, viii
spirit beings. *See* persons other than human
stepfathers, 53, 54
stepmothers, 53, 54
Stocking, George W., Jr., xiii
Stoney, Peter, 36
structures, ceremonial, 74, 84
Sturgeon lineages, 23 map, 24
Sun, 64, 66, 74
    as animate being, 61
"sweethearts," 55–56, 95

T
taboos, 52, 65, 67, 88, 92
technology, aboriginal, 33
territoriality. *See* hunting territories
Thunder Birds, 61–62, 64, 66–67, 70–71
    human communication with, 70–71
time, concepts of, 4, 73–74
trade goods, 18, 25–26
treaties
    Selkirk-Cree-Ojibwa, 1817, 21
    Treaty 1, Canada-Cree-Ojibwa, 1871, 32,
        35
    Treaty 5 (Lake Winnipeg), Canada-Cree-
        Ojibwa, 1875, 3 map, 13, 32–33, 33–
        35, 36–37
Turtles, Big, 61, 65

U

underworld, 74
usufruct. *See* customary use

V

Verendrye, Pierre Gaultier de Varennes, 11
violence as cause of illness, 95

W

Wabanowiwin, 9, 12, 70–71, 75 ill., 84
windigowak (persons other than human), 64–
   65
   in shaking tent, 70
winds, 64, 66
   as animate beings, 61
   birth of, 74
   North, 66, 74
   South, 66
Winnipeg in 1860s and 1870s, 31–32
Wisekedjak (person other than human), 71,
   73
   and metamorphosis, 67

witchcraft, 95–96
The Wolverine (lake boat), 7 ill.
women
   avoidance of, 88
   and blessings, 88
   and dreams, 88, 114
   as healers, 98n.3
   lack of information about, 114
   marriage of to persons other than human,
      67
   and menopause, 88
   occupations of, 9, 18, 49, 88, 102, 114
   and power, 88, 114
   and toothed vaginas, 73
   and use of plants, 9, 98n.3
world, shape of, 74

Y

Yellow Legs (c.1750–c.1830), 11–12, 22
   and shaking tent, 68
Young, E. Ryerson, xii
Young, Egerton R., xii, 13, 29, 35